THE JOHN DEWEY LECTURE

The John Dewey Lecture has been delivered annually since 1958 under the sponsorship of the John Dewey Society. The intention of the series is to provide a setting where able thinkers from various sectors of our intellectual life can direct their most searching thoughts to problems that involve the relation of education to culture. Arrangements for the presentation of the Lecture and its publication by Teachers College Press are under the direction of Daniel Tanner, Chairperson.

RECENT TITLES IN THE SERIES

Excellence in Public Discourse:
John Stuart Mill, John Dewey, and Social Intelligence
James Gouinlock

Building a Global Civic Culture:
Education for an Interdependent World
Elise Boulding

The Dialectic of Freedom
Maxine Greene

Education for Intelligent Belief or Unbelief
Nel Noddings

Cultural Politics and Education
Michael W. Apple

In Praise of Education
John I. Goodlad

John Dewey and the Philosopher's Task
Philip W. Jackson

Cultural Miseducation:
In Search of a Democratic Solution
Jane Roland Martin

Cultural
Miseducation

IN SEARCH OF A DEMOCRATIC SOLUTION

Jane Roland Martin

Teachers College, Columbia University
New York and London

Published by Teachers College Press, 1234 Amsterdam Avenue, New York, NY 10027

The cultural wealth perspective presented in Chapters 1 and 2 was first put forward in "There's Too Much to Teach" in *Educational Researcher, 25*, 4–10, 16. Copyright 1996 by the American Educational Research Association. Adapted with permission of the publisher.

Portions of Chapter 3 are reprinted from "The Wealth of Cultures and the Problem of Generations," in *Philosophy of Education*, edited by S. Tozer, 1999, Urbana, IL: Philosophy of Education Society. Copyright 1999 by the Philosophy of Education Society. Reprinted by permission of the publisher.

Portions of Chapter 5 appeared under the title "The New Problem of Curriculum" in 1993 in *Synthese, 94*, 85–104. Copyright 1993 by Kluwer Academic Publishers. Adapted with kind permission from Kluwer Academic Publishers.

Library of Congress Cataloging-in-Publication Data

Martin, Jane Roland, 1929–
    Cultural miseducation : in search of a democratic solution / Jane Roland Martin.
      p. cm. — (The John Dewey lecture)
    Includes bibliographical references and index.
    ISBN 0-8077-4239-2 (pbk. : alk. paper) — ISBN 0-8077-4240-6 (cloth : alk. paper)
    1. Education—Social aspects—United States.   2. Multicultural education—United States.   3. Progressive education—United States. I. Title. II. John Dewey lecture (Teachers College Press)

LC191.4 .M36 2002
370.11'5—dc21   2002016174

ISBN 0-8077-4239-2 (paper)
ISBN 0-8077-4240-6 (cloth)

Printed on acid-free paper
Manufactured in the United States of America

09 08 07 06 05 04 03 02   8 7 6 5 4 3 2 1

For the new generation of Martins:
Maxwell Oliver, Gabriel Ethan, and Zachary Charles

Contents

Foreword

A CENTURY AGO John Dewey began to articulate his principles for a democratic society. Among them was his belief that a full-flowering democracy is rooted in the soil of community. Only when individual citizens see themselves as part of the greater community are they likely to share cooperatively their various interests, abilities, and attainments for the good of society as a whole. The more deeply they participate in society's ongoing dialogue among its many different members about beliefs, values, and actions, the more likely they are to experience a growing sense of community, and democracy itself grows. Democracy, Dewey thought, both depends on and fosters the fullest and most intelligent participation of all members of a community.

Applied to schools, these principles wrought a revolution. The story is well known. Rather than schools being places where all students were expected to learn the same things, schools could become—and many did become—democratic communities nurturing shared activities and cooperation among students, teachers, parents, principals, school boards, and interested citizens. Teachers could act as guides, suggesting individual or group projects that students could shape as their own. Everyone could participate in decisions about what might be taught or learned. Such schools taught democracy to students primarily because such schools embodied a democratic culture.

Today, at the beginning of the 21st century, schools are under intense pressure to become less democratic. Thinly disguised by the banners of excellence and equality and espoused by politicians wielding financial carrots and financial sticks, the seductive specters of social efficiency, uniform standards, high-stakes testing, and misapplied accountability stalk the American landscape and dominate public debate about what education should be. The struggle is not much different than it was in Dewey's day, when one prominent spokesperson for authoritarianism in education crassly but clearly stated his notion of school reform:

> In any organization, the directive and supervisory members must clearly define the ends toward which the organization strives. They must co-ordinate the labors of all so as to attain those ends. They must find the best methods of work, and they must enforce the use of these methods on the part of the workers. (John Franklin Bobbitt, *The Supervision of City Schools*, 1913, p. 7)

In CULTURAL MISEDUCATION, Jane Roland Martin rebuts the current challenge to the Deweyan tradition even as she moves beyond the emphasis Dewey placed in *Democracy and Education* (1916) on schools and the growth and development of individuals. The problems of education are not confined to schooling, she points out, for society at large educates in numerous ways, some planned, but most unplanned. Beginning with the truism that culture is too vast to be entirely transmitted to future generations and noting that culture itself is composed of what she calls "cultural wealth"and "cultural liabilities,"she confronts the age-old, vexing problem of how to maximize the transmission of the former while minimizing the transmission of the latter.

For schools, no solution lies in adopting a single, uniform curriculum, no matter how wisely selected its various parts might be. Such a curriculum inevitably becomes elitist, she explains, even though—ironically— usually justified as egalitarian. Furthermore, even if it were to avoid transmitting any cultural liabilities, it would still always fail to transmit large measures of the cultural wealth.

Her preferred solution? That lies in a new conception of community, which she develops throughout the book. Along the way, as she confronts the specters of antidemocratic education and articulates her view of what a community can be, there are many fresh insights and wonderful, full-fleshed examples that substantiate her views.

Her touch is deft; her analyses are sure. Prepare to see the most basic problem of education and cultural regeneration in a new light.

—George Willis, for the John Dewey Society

Acknowledgments

THIS VOLUME represents the fruits of the project for which I was awarded a fellowship by the John Simon Guggenheim Memorial Foundation in 1987. I am eternally grateful to the foundation for supporting my work on education at a critical moment in my professional life.

I need hardly add that in the intervening years my Guggenheim project took unexpected twists and turns. One of these led to the cultural-wealth approach to education that informs this book from beginning to end. I first put forward this perspective in my 1995 DeGarmo Lecture, presented at the national meeting of the American Educational Research Association. Here I wish to thank the Society of Professors of Education for inviting me to give that address and the editors of *Educational Researcher* for publishing "There's Too Much to Teach: Cultural Wealth in an Age of Scarcity" (Martin, 1996). My thanks go also to the John Dewey Society for naming me the John Dewey Lecturer for 1996 and to Teachers College Press for publishing this book in its John Dewey Lecture Series. I can think of no greater honor.

Just as Chapters 1 and 2 of this book draw heavily on the discussion of cultural wealth and multiple educational agency in my DeGarmo Lecture, they draw on the analysis of the poverty of our culture's concept of education contained in the Dewey Lecture I gave at the national meeting of the American Educational Research Association and then at Teachers College. After that Dewey Lecture there was another turning point in the evolution of this work. For the opportunity to develop and receive feedback on my new formulation of the old problem of generations, an idea now central to the book as a whole and explicitly explored in Chapter 3, I wish to thank two groups: the Department of Philosophy and College of Arts and Sciences at Oswego State University, under whose auspices in 1998 I delivered the Eleventh Annual Warren Steinkraus Lecture on Human

Ideals entitled "The Ideal of an Educative Society"; and the Philosophy of Education Society, which that same year sponsored my Distinguished Guest Lecture "The Wealth of Cultures and the Problem of Generations" at its national meeting and then published it in the society's *Proceedings* (Martin, 1999).

Let me also thank Jaakko Hintikka, editor of *Synthese*, for his invitation to write a paper for his journal's special issue honoring Israel Scheffler. "The New Problem of Curriculum" (Martin, 1993) represents my first formulation in print of the problem at the heart of my Guggenheim proposal and now at the center of Chapter 5. My thanks go also to the Philosophy of Education Society of Great Britain and its then vice-chair, Patricia White, for inviting me to read a paper at the group's 1993 conference in Oxford entitled "The Problem of Curricular Abundance," in which I elaborated those early ideas. In addition, I am grateful to Joshua Cohen, editor of the *Boston Review*, for publishing in the February/March 1995 issue of that periodical the short piece "Cultural Citizenship," which informs the last section of Chapter 4; and to Margaret Crocco for organizing the symposium "Civic Education and Cultural Citizenship" at the 1996 annual meeting of the American Educational Research Association.

As ever, I wish to thank Ann Diller, Susan Franzosa, Barbara Houston, Michael Martin, Beatrice Nelson, Jennifer Radden, and Janet Farrell Smith for reading selected sections of earlier drafts of my manuscript and discussing the ideas contained therein with me. Finally, I am beholden to Barbara Houston, Susan Laird, Michael Martin, Maurice Stein, Mary Woods, and an anonymous reviewer for Teachers College Press for reading the entire manuscript and giving me extremely helpful comments and advice, and to Michael Martin for supporting me and my project at every step along the way.

Cultural
Miseducation

Introduction

"WHY ARE YOU so worried about the cultural heritage?" asked a friend when I told her the subject of this book. "Isn't that an item on the conservative agenda?" I said to her—and I say it again here—that what a culture passes down to the next generation is everyone's business.

Plato, one of history's most profound thinkers, knew this. A fundamental insight in his *Republic* was that if left to its own devices, society is apt to transmit cultural liabilities to the next generation instead of cultural wealth. Two of his favorite examples of liabilities were cowardice and impiety. Two of mine are violence, be it at home or school, in the local neighborhood or the world at large; and hatred, be it of other races, religions, genders, ethnicities, or sexual orientations. The issue here, however, is not which cultural liabilities are the worst. The issue is that despite the importance of Plato's insight, his solution to the problem of miseducation is unacceptable. Quite simply, the thoroughgoing system of censorship he offered as a solution to cultural miseducation runs counter to the principles of democracy.

Jean-Jacques Rousseau, who in 1762 wrote that the *Republic* is the most beautiful educational treatise ever written, also knew that what a culture passes along is everyone's business. The reason that the hero of his own educational masterpiece, *Émile,* is removed at birth from his family and placed under the care of a tutor in virtual isolation is that Rousseau considered society to be miseducative in the extreme. But although Rousseau correctly diagnosed the problem, his solution to it was as flawed as Plato's. To avoid the evils that occur when cultural liabilities are passed down to future generations, this father of democracy devised his own full-blown system of social control. Plato placed authority over the lives of the populace in the hands of an all-knowing ruling class. Rousseau took it away from those philosopher kings and queens and gave total dominion instead to

1

an all-powerful tutor whose duty it was to determine every detail of his charge's environment and to monitor the boy's every move.

No doubt one reason that education's recent critics and reformers have ignored the problem of cultural miseducation is that undemocratic solutions such as Plato's and Rousseau's come so readily to mind. Even when the violence and hatred, the poverty and greed that are being passed down threaten to tear the very fabric of society, it may in their eyes seem far better to suffer cultural miseducation than to institute totalitarian remedies. This avoidance behavior might be justified if democratic solutions to our problem were impossible to envision. But as I will try to show in the course of developing a "cultural-wealth" approach to education, the pessimism is unwarranted.

Quite aside from issues of totalitarianism, it is all too easy to disregard the problem of cultural miseducation. That is because most of us take it for granted that the proper way to think about education is to adopt the standpoint of the individual. Parents ask: Is my child learning in school what she (or he) needs to know? Psychologists ask: How does a child construct knowledge? What forms of intelligence does he or she possess? Philosophers ask, What is an educated person? What does a citizen of a democracy need to know?

Sometimes the scope of the question is broadened. In his classic *The Souls of Black Folk*, W. E. B. DuBois (1903/1965) asked: What does the "Negro race" need to learn to be socially "uplifted"? In her groundbreaking treatise *A Vindication of the Rights of Woman*, Mary Wollstonecraft (1792/ 1967) asked: What kind of education must women have to become the equals of men? More recently, educational researchers have asked: How do girls experience the coeducational classroom climate? What do high school graduates need to know? Sometimes schools or school districts are placed in the limelight: Which Boston area school ranks first on reading proficiency? Which community ranks last? But in the final analysis even these queries are fueled by a concern about children's learning.

There is another way to look at education, however. Instead of concentrating on the achievements—or, in the event, the failures—of individuals or groups, one can take the standpoint of the culture. Be forewarned that looking at education from this vantage point for the first time can be an unsettling experience. At the start one may not see anything at all. After a while, what appeared to be a blank canvas becomes populated with educational phenomena. Linger long enough at this cultural vantage point and one perceives that whole societies are educative—or miseducative, as the case may be. Institutions of every imaginable sort begin to loom large as the preservers and transmitters of cultural wealth: schools, of course, but also libraries and museums, churches and synagogues, American

Indian tribes and African American communities, business and banks, magazines and television, et cetera, et cetera, et cetera. And above all, new questions suddenly seem pressing. Is the culture preserving its assets for the next generation? Are some assets—for instance, farm skills, American Indian languages and dances, household arts, Asian American history and literature, alternative ways of responding to aggression, Mexican American family structures and traditions—getting lost in transmission? Are cultural liabilities being transmitted? Issues like these are everyone's business.

The cultural-wealth perspective I put forward in this book was many years in the making. Throughout that 15-year period the question on people's minds was whether the traditional school curriculum was sufficient unto the day or whether the new conditions of society required that new subjects be added to the old—for instance, women's history, African American literature, the treatment of American Indians, Asian and Hispanic studies, the immigrant experience. I am on record as advocating an inclusionary school curriculum (Martin, 1992). Here, after addressing some basic questions that those end-of-the-twentieth-century curriculum debates ignored, I place this issue in a new light.

How is a culture's wealth to be defined? I say that it cannot legitimately be reduced to "high" culture, as many people seem to think. Rather, it includes the whole range of human activities. Who is qualified to contribute to the wealth? I say that all members of a culture—not just some privileged racial, religious, gendered, or other elite—have this right. What agencies besides school preserve and transmit the wealth? I say that all the institutions and informal groupings of society are guardians of a culture's wealth, and hence its educational agents. How well do the custodians do their jobs? In particular, do they transmit liabilities as well as assets? My examination of such fundamentals as these leads directly to my formulation of what is surely one of the most important problems to face any culture or society: How do we maximize the transmission of cultural wealth and at the same time minimize the transmission of cultural liabilities. A solution to this "educational problem of generations" requires close study of the claim that democracy mandates one curriculum for everybody.

There is no doubt about it. Whether a person tends toward inclusion or exclusion in matters of curriculum—whether he or she favors or opposes the teaching of Toni Morrison's novels, Virginia Woolf's feminist essays, American Indian myths and literature—to approve the policy of a single curriculum for all is to restrict radically the amount of cultural wealth that is passed down to the next generation. Yet is the alternative of different curricula for different people compatible with democracy? Does it not run counter to the ideals of social equality and individual self-government? I say that it is compatible *provided* we rethink some basic assumptions about learning, about knowledge, and about social relationships.

The issues that emerge when a cultural perspective on education is taken are profound, and the questions to which they give rise admit of no easy answers. Perhaps nowhere is evidence of this perspective so readily discernible as in the first pages of John Dewey's magnum opus, *Democracy and Education*. "Society exists through a process of transmission quite as much as biological life," wrote Dewey in that 1916 treatise. Saying "the fact that some are born as some die, makes possible through transmission of ideas and practices the constant reweaving of the social fabric," he added that the renewal cannot be taken for granted: "Unless pains are taken to see that genuine and thorough transmission takes place, the most civilized group will relapse into barbarism and then into savagery" (Dewey, 1916/ 1961, pp. 3–4). Yet as one reads on, Dewey's interest in the transmission of culture from one generation to the next gives way to an individualistic perspective. True, in his philosophy individual human beings are thoroughly social creatures and community plays a central role. Nevertheless, despite those opening remarks, the main focus of *Democracy and Education* is the growth and development of individuals.

Although he said in the opening pages of *Democracy and Education* that school is but one method of cultural transmission and "a relatively superficial means" at that (Dewey, 1916/1961, p. 4), Dewey's focus was also on schools. Why exactly he allowed school to take over his text is something of a mystery, but one thing is clear. Had he retained his initial emphasis on cultural transmission, school would not have been able to capture center stage of *Democracy and Education*. It has certainly been my experience that one who looks at education from a cultural point of view will eventually start scanning the landscape to see what institutions besides school are dedicated to preserving and transmitting the vast amount of cultural wealth. I also know firsthand that one who acknowledges the amazing array of educational agents in our midst will soon discover that many of these institutions are more adept at passing down cultural liabilities than assets to our young.

Now it must be said that generations have pored over the works of Plato, Rousseau, and Dewey—arguably the three greatest figures in the West's history of educational thought—without being converted to a cultural-wealth approach to education. For more years than I care to count, I myself was one of those who had read these men's writings without really grasping the importance of a cultural perspective. Things changed when I began doing research on the education of girls and women.

My conversion to a cultural perspective was a gradual process. It has long been a commonplace that women are the ones who pass down a culture's values to the next generation. Nonetheless, when I wrote *Reclaiming a Conversation* (Martin, 1985), a book about the education of women, the idea of cultural wealth was the furthest thing from my mind. Still and all, on the day I started to think of women as the culture's custodians of the knowledge, skills, and values pertaining to the world of the private home, my conversion to the cultural-wealth approach to education I present here was under way.

As a philosopher of education, I was accustomed to reading academic texts. But after publication of *Reclaiming a Conversation*, I began to study the culture's patterns of thought about school and home in addition to the writings of educational theorists and philosophers. In the short run this exercise in cultural anthropology led to my unearthing the complex set of tacit cultural assumptions about education that I enumerated in *The Schoolhome* (Martin, 1992). In the long run it enabled me to develop a cultural-wealth approach to education. This latter led, in turn, to my recognition of the problem of cultural miseducation. By this I mean that societies—and also groups and institutions within them—can be educative, but they can also be sadly miseducative. Cultural miseducation occurs when so many cultural liabilities or such devastating ones are passed down that a heavy burden is placed on the next generation; or, alternatively, when invaluable portions of the culture's wealth are not passed down. And, of course, it occurs when these sins of omission and commission are conjoined.

It must also be stressed that one need not have read Plato, Rousseau, or Dewey to be concerned about the problem of cultural miseducation. Throughout history, countless individuals have documented aspects of this phenomenon, albeit without ever giving it this name.

One of the turning points in his life, said Malcolm X in his autobiography, was when a teacher who had internalized the culture's messages about the "Negro" said to him:

> Don't misunderstand me, now. We all here like you, you know that. But you've got to be realistic about being a nigger. A lawyer—that's no realistic goal for a nigger. You need to think about something you can be. You're good with your hands—making things. Everybody admires your carpentry shop work. Why don't you plan on carpentry? People like you as a person—you'd get all kinds of work. (1966, p. 36)

Looking back on her childhood, a Mexican American writer recalled that her sisters "were ashamed to take tortilla tacos [to school] for lunch. They were afraid the gringos would laugh and say nasty things. We still tried to hide our Mexicanness, not believing yet that it was impossible" (E. Hart, 1999, p. 26). An American Indian scholar wrote:

> The view of Indians as hostile savages who capture white ladies and torture them, obstruct the westward movement of peaceable white settlers, and engage in bloodthirsty uprisings in which they glory in the massacre of innocent colonists and pioneers is dear to the hearts of producers of bad films and even worse television. However, it is a view that is most deeply embedded in the American unconscious. (Allen, 1986, p. 5)

And feminist scholars across the board have demonstrated that the lives and works of women of all races, classes, ethnicities, and sexual orientations are either missing from the disciplines of knowledge or are misrepresented therein.

Since, however, the works of Plato, Rousseau, and Dewey contain the seeds of the philosophy of education I develop here, I will introduce some of their ideas into the discussion as I proceed. But let me emphasize that I do not regard these men as authority figures whose pronouncements cannot be questioned. Rather, I cite their ideas to provide a context—a neglected philosophical tradition, if you will—in which to frame the present study.

As a case in point, consider Dewey's brief affirmation of the importance of cultural transmission. Taking it far more seriously than he himself did, the approach to education I will set forth in these pages reinforces his caveat about school. I trust that what I have to say will do much more than this, however, for in sowing and nurturing those seeds that Plato first planted, I am trying to bring to fruition a new way of thinking about that thing called education.

My object is not to replace or discredit the traditional focus on individuals but to supplement it with a different, equally important perspective. I need hardly say how disastrous it would be to forget that individual students and teachers, parents and children participate in education. This inquiry into the problem of cultural miseducation and search for a democratic solution will show that it is just as dangerous to lose sight of the other elements of the educational equation. It will also show why the disposal of the culture's wealth—indeed, of its assets *and* liabilities—is the business of every man, woman, and child.

CHAPTER 1

Cultural Wealth

ABUNDANCE; OR, THERE'S TOO MUCH TO TEACH

At a conference on excellence in education I once attended, a member of the audience interrupted the speaker to ask what he should stop teaching the kids in his classes. "We can't do everything we're supposed to, and you're telling us to do more," this distraught man shouted. When the speaker was slow to respond, someone else jumped up and said, "I can answer your question. We've got to cut out the trivia and just teach what's important." As it happened, he thought that philosophy was important whereas the speaker leaned toward history. Much to the disappointment of a group of listeners whose wandering attention had become riveted on the unfolding drama, the relative merits of history and philosophy were not debated. Nor was the original question joined.

Surely I was not alone in regretting the speaker's decision to get on with her lecture instead of taking time out to comment on the brute fact of cultural abundance. I cannot have been the only person to wish that she had seen fit to explore its accompanying problem of curriculum selection. Almost every schoolteacher has at one time or another been driven to the brink by the thought of how much there is to teach and how impossible it is to do it all. Just about every child has wondered at least once or twice why he or she was being told to learn this rather than that.

The speaker's unwillingness to engage the question made me realize just how uncomfortable the brute fact of cultural abundance makes educators, and for good reason. It is much easier to forget that there is too much to teach than to wonder if something other than Plato's *Republic*, long division, Patrick Henry, and the U.S. state capitals should have been included in the course of study. One who never asks "What should be taught?" will feel no guilt about exposing the next generation to only a small portion of our cultural heritage. One who overlooks how much wealth there is will never know how little of the cultural inheritance he or she has actually acquired.

Memory loss regarding how much there is to teach the next generation is aided and abetted by the fact that the world has become accustomed to a framework of thought whose fundamental premise is scarcity. In the case of culture, however, the issue is abundance. Humankind is used to there being too little wealth to distribute, but in this instance there is too much. Our vast cultural resources are what make the question of what to teach so pressing. The query that has often been called "the" question of curriculum—namely, What should be taught?—is appallingly difficult to answer precisely because the pool of potential subject matter is so large that no one can hope to teach everything in it. Nor can a single individual hope to master it all.

How paradoxical that even as so many of the world's resources have been shrinking, the inheritance from which curriculum's content is drawn has been growing! The problem of curriculum selection is becoming ever more pressing not just because information has accumulated over the years. As one commentator has said, there are now "dozens and dozens of disciplines, each one nearly a separate nation with its own governance, psychology entelechy" (Ozick, 1987). Within each discipline there are also now dozens and dozens of perspectives. In addition, researchers have begun to find out about the works, experiences, practices, and achievements of people who have always been part of society but have never quite been acknowledged as members of culture.

It is unlikely that my intrepid junior high school teacher had in mind the burgeoning scholarship on women, African Americans, Native Americans, gays and lesbians, poor people, the differently abled, Hispanic and Asian Americans when he protested that there was too much to teach. Nevertheless, as a visit to any bookstore or a tour of the Internet will testify, since 1970 an enormous amount of work has been done in these areas.

I realize that the blossoming of the relatively new studies does not guarantee their worth. I also know that even as new wealth was once compared unfavorably to old, this new scholarship is devalued. It used to be said that old economic wealth has proved itself stable, reliable, enduring—in other words, trustworthy—whereas new wealth is subject to the whim of the moment, hence unreliable and short lived. I also recall being told that the sources of the new economic wealth and its manner of acquisition tainted it. According to my informants—my *mis*informants, as it turned out—the old wealth was honestly earned in enterprises designed to benefit the general welfare whereas the motive for the new wealth was personal gain and no holds had been barred in the course of getting it.

The superior reputation of old scholarship also rests on its staying power. If a literary work or scientific theory were frivolous or untrustworthy, how could it possibly have passed the test of time? If its point of view were anything other than universal and objective, how could it still speak to the experience of all of us? Moreover, it has often been said that the way those old theories and narratives were arrived at was exemplary. Did not their authors set all bias aside in order to be disinterested, impartial spectators of both man and nature? And do not the very names of the newer scholarly fields—*Native American* Studies, *Women's* Studies, *Gay and Lesbian* Studies, and the rest—reflect the limited standpoints of their researchers and serve notice that their findings are arbitrary and subjective?

I became deeply disillusioned when the claims of old economic wealth turned out to be as flawed as Henry James's golden bowl. The case for the old established theories and narratives also shatters along its fault lines. Those supposedly universal theories of human development depicted the development of White, middle-class men and boys. Those presumably objective standards of great literature were abstracted from the study of works by male, not female, human beings. Those purportedly neutral fields of history and politics defined their subject matter so as to exclude the lives and experiences of most women and many men.

In addition, just as the old economic wealth was eventually exposed as the loot of robber barons who exploited their workers, cheated their customers, bribed politicians, and waged war on their competitors, the creation of the scholarship of yore has been shown to depend on unacknowledged, unrewarded labor. No strike breaking, to be sure, and no company towns. But the new social studies of science report that the Royal Societies opened their doors only to White men and that scientific laboratories are hierarchical institutions whose heads are mainly White men and whose menial laborers are mainly women and non-White men. Literary and historical studies of women leave no doubt, either, as to who did the typing, the clerical work, and of course the housework for all those humanistic scholars who never set foot in a laboratory.

One big difference between economic wealth and scholarship is that the latter can self-consciously reflect back on earlier instances of itself. Besides shedding light on the origins of the early scholarship, the new research has revealed that the authors of the old were not quite so disinterested and impartial as we have been led to believe. Rereading and reinterpreting the theories and narratives that were put forward as explanations of human behavior, human development, and human intelligence, recent investigations have discovered that those products apply only to White, middle-class males.

But now a puzzle arises: By its very existence, today's scholarship increases our cultural stock, yet in the very act of looking backward it has managed to diminish the value of much of the old. One way to prevent this loss is to pretend that the new work does not exist. I would say, however, that it is far better to acknowledge the limitations of those earlier achievements. Theories that falsely generalize can dangerously mislead and narratives that trade in stereotypes can cruelly deceive. Besides, the new scholarship is doubly valuable. It constitutes new stock and also recovers cultural assets that have over time been lost to us—the activities of 17th-century midwives and the diaries of slaves, for instance.

It would be a terrible mistake, however, to suppose that the world today has mislaid or forgotten only those portions of cultural stock that relate to women and minorities or, worse still, to conclude that our culture's stock consists only of books. When I read Wendell Berry's essays on farming—in particular, his description of the activities and attitudes of a good farmer of "the old school"—I thought mainly about the old agricultural knowledge and skill, attitudes and perspectives that are now at risk. I also wondered how much has already been forgotten and how much of that is perhaps irretrievable. During a trip to Ireland where he visited farms, walked through pastures, and talked at length to farmers, Berry wrote in his journal: "One would like to know how many people there are left in the Irish countryside who could build or 'lay' a hedge" (1987, p. 35). Referring to field gates of wrought iron that were shopmade, he said: "And one hopes that they will be studied and understood, not as relics but as valuable cultural and agricultural achievements, before they are gone. If they can be so understood, they will be preserved and, beyond that, imitated" (p. 41).

Yet a practically minded person might ask what difference it makes if the know-how to construct a wrought-iron field gate or to lay a hedge is lost to us. What difference if a 105-year-old medicine man with extensive knowledge of the healing properties of Amazon rain-forest plants dies and leaves no apprentices. What difference if the 19th-century domestic novels written by women are not read in school. Is it not to be expected that knowledge, skills, artforms handed down from artisan to apprentice, farmer to son, midwife to daughter, choreographer to dancer, publisher to reader will finally be forgotten? Surely, what counts as vital know-how in one historical period is quite irrelevant to another. Surely, one of the main virtues of an advanced civilization is that it liberates us from the techniques of the past. Or does it? After citing the many ways in which disputes throughout history have been resolved without violence, the author of a textbook in Peace Studies wrote: "We are surrounded with subliminal messages that peacemaking is an impossible dream, whereas warmaking—or at best deterrence—is the only reality" (Barash, 1991, p. 30).

The truth is that one never knows enough about old forgotten traditions and practices to be sure that there is nothing more to be learned from them. Nor can one know what the future will bring. A once-precious skill or practice may now be unusable. An idea or concept developed at an earlier time will seem irrelevant to our present plight. Yet who knows what might be gleaned from this relic today, tomorrow, or 50 years hence. Who can say that at a later date or perhaps right now we cannot adapt it to good advantage.

"You sound just like a child of the Depression," a young friend said when I told her why cultural stock is worth preserving. "My grandmother even had a box on her shelf labeled 'String Too Short to Use.'"

I agree that thrift can be carried too far, but I am also aware that new ways of doing things often have devastating effects. In the 1970s the Indonesian government forced rice farmers in Bali to adopt new agricultural methods. The results were disastrous (Fountain, 2000, p. 5). The introduction of the eucalyptus into arid regions of India as an efficient source of pulp has destroyed the water cycles (Shiva, 1993). Peru, whose agriculturalists by the time of the Spanish Conquest grew about 3000 varieties of potato and had perfected the first freeze-dried method of preserving the potato, now has to import potatoes from the Netherlands in order to feed its people (Weatherford, 1993, p. 67).

In saying one never knows when it will come in handy, I do not mean to suggest that *every* bit of cultural stock should be preserved. So far as I am concerned, racism, poverty, terrorism, child abuse, lynching, wife beating, and physical and psychological torture are cultural practices that should not under any circumstances be handed down as living legacies to future generations. But this is not to say that we should refrain from passing down knowledge *about* them. How else are we to keep past mistakes from being repeated?

Just as it is an error to turn one's back on the wealth generated by the new scholarship, it is imprudent to dismiss old, indigenous practices and know-how out of hand. Even as I was rehearsing my reasons for preserving this wealth, an international news service announced a new study by anthropologists and ecologists recommending a return to the tilling methods used by pre-Columbian farmers in the Andes. Two weeks later, bold headlines reported that a Tibetan now living in Massachusetts had used ancient stone-working skills to restore a charcoal kiln, one of the last remaining structures of an extinct New England industry.

DEFINING THE WEALTH;
OR, A MISCHIEVOUS REDUCTION

"I have the solution to your problem of There's Too Much to Teach," a literary scholar told me as I was starting to write this book. "Whatever I can't fit into my lectures I put on the reading list." Her surprise when I explained what to me was so obvious—that our cultural wealth does not fit on even the most extensive reading list—told me that she was implicitly operating under neat but far too narrow definitions of both culture and curriculum.

When in 1776 the Scottish philosopher Adam Smith inquired into the wealth of nations, he was as concerned with its nature as its causes. "That wealth consists in money, or in gold and silver, is a popular notion which naturally arises from the double function of money, as the instrument of commerce and as a measure of value," he said in Volume I of his treatise on the topic (1776/1976, p. 450). Indeed, the definition of wealth as money was such a commonplace in his day that, in Smith's view, even the great philosopher David Hume had not sufficiently questioned it. "It would be too ridiculous to go about seriously to prove, that wealth does not consist in money, or in gold and silver; but in what money purchases, and is valuable for purchasing," Smith wrote (p. 459). Reminding readers that *An Inquiry into the Nature and Causes of the Wealth of Nations* was doing the ridiculous, he added: "Money, no doubt, makes always a part of the national capital; but it has already been shown that it generally makes but a small part, and always the most unprofitable part of it" (p. 459).

That cultural wealth consists entirely of "high" culture—or perhaps more accurately of "high" culture and the "higher" learning—is as popular a notion at the start of the 21st century as the confusion of money, or gold and silver, with wealth was in 18th-century England. It is presupposed when someone refers to an acquaintance as a highly cultured person. It is assumed in debates about whether Boston qualifies as a seat of culture. And it is a given in all those accusations that school is failing to pass down the cultural heritage to the next generation.

It has rightly been said that Smith democratized the concept of a nation's economic wealth by broadening the definition to include not just the wealth of kings, or even the wealth of the merchant class, but the goods that *all* people in a society consume (Heilbroner, 1953). In rejecting narrow definitions of cultural wealth as "high" culture or the "higher" learning, I democratize this analogous concept. Of course, it would be ridiculous to deny that the acknowledged masterpieces of Western civilization are a part of our cultural wealth. But there is far more to a culture's wealth than the acknowledged classics of art, music, and literature; more even than these together with philosophy and economics, history and literature, science and psychology.

Culture in the broadest sense of the term includes not just artistic and scholarly products, whether masterpieces or works of lesser merit. It encompasses the institutions and practices, rites and rituals, beliefs and skills, attitudes and values, worldviews and localized modes of thinking and acting of *all* members of society over the *whole* range of contexts. Not everything in a culture's stock counts as *wealth*, of course, for the term *wealth*, like the term *riches*, carries with it a positive assessment. But it is a far cry from acknowledging that a culture's *stock* consists in liabilities as well as assets to the assumption that "high" culture and the "higher" learning exhaust its riches.

The sense of culture—and by extension cultural wealth—that I would substitute for the reductive one is akin to the anthropologist's. When anthropologists study cultures, they do not dream of limiting their sights to some small subset of practices and accomplishments. They do not even restrict themselves to something resembling what has come to be called "popular" culture—the art, music, literature, humor, sporting events that are consumed by ordinary people. Nor do they focus exclusively on the tools and other artifacts that comprise material culture. Their definitions of culture as "all learned behavior"—or, alternately, as "the whole range of human activities which are learned and not instinctive" (Herskovits, 1952, p. 21; Beattie, 1964, p. 20)—encompass whatever might correspond to our own conceptions of high, popular, and material culture, but they embrace countless other items, too. An old farmer's know-how, an artisan's craft, a mother's daily lessons to her offspring in the three Cs of care, concern, and connection are all, therefore, grist for an anthropologist's mill. As cultural assets, these also fall squarely in the category of cultural wealth; and so, presumably, do the "products" of these practices.

But now another puzzle arises. In Western thought culture and nature have commonly been defined in opposition to each other. Thus, nature is said to be whatever is untouched by human hands or whatever is independent of the actions of humanity. Yet when cultural practices are broadly defined, some of their products or outcomes would seem to be a part of nature's bounty. Think of the fruits of agriculture. Think of hunting and fishing, sheep herding and cattle raising. For that matter, think of zoos, aquariums, national parks, gardens, arboretums.

Actually, when nature is defined in sharp contrast to culture, neither bird, beast, nor fish—neither wind, sun, nor rain—belongs to nature. Anyone who doubts that the fingerprints of humankind are everywhere should consider this: "The average American car driven the average American distance—ten thousand miles—in an average American year releases its own weight in carbon into the atmosphere" (McKibben, 1989, p. 6). And this:

> If you'd climbed some remote mountain in 1960 and sealed up a bottle of air at its peak, and did the same thing this year, the two samples would be substantially different. Their basic chemistry would have changed. (McKibben, 1989, p. 18)

Solar warming, acid rain, and the ease with which bears break into automobiles at Yosemite National Park testify to culture's influence on nature. And the idea of a human culture totally insulated from the influences of the so-called natural world of wind, sun, and rain is not borne out by the facts either. Think of Shelley's "Ode to the West Wind." Think of Debussy's *La Mer*. Surely, when what everyone agrees are natural processes do not fall under the common definition of nature, and when the idea of a nature-free culture has no more validity than that of a natural world completely insulated from human culture, the time has come to abandon the sharp nature–culture dichotomy that has for centuries informed Western thought.

In recent years Western philosophers have begun to characterize the nature–culture relationship as a matter of degree rather than as a difference of kind. Since the new mappings of the relationship differ considerably in their details, I consider it the better part of wisdom to take no stand on their relative adequacy here. From a logical point of view this strategy is also warranted: In order to make the definition of cultural wealth coherent, the only thing required is that the overlap between the two categories be acknowledged.

When the definition of cultural wealth is democratized, questions arise not only about the relationship of culture to nature, but also about the basis for distinguishing assets from liabilities and for determining whether some particular item of cultural stock represents asset or liability. Questions arise, too, about the value that attaches to different categories of cultural wealth, how this last is to be decided, and by whom.

Whenever I have presented my ideas on a cultural-wealth approach to education, these have been the questions on the audience's minds. And rightly so, for people across the globe disagree about whether, for example, religious pluralism, the education of women, poverty, war, and social inequality are cultural assets or liabilities. Nonetheless, value issues such as these are not the creatures of a cultural-wealth approach to education. On the contrary, our culture—indeed, any culture—confronts them whether or not it looks at education from a cultural perspective. Although they desperately need to be resolved, their resolution need not occur prior to the development of a cultural-wealth approach to education. In fact, if it were really essential to decide the pertinent value issues before delineating this new perspective, our endeavor might never get off the ground. They are so difficult to answer and their answers tend to be so controversial, it is a foregone conclusion that whatever answers are given will be found wanting.

As a case in point, consider the claim made by a prominent cultural critic that weaving and jazz are lesser arts than oil painting, opera, and ballet (Henry, 1994). His basis for so saying was that the latter are more intellectual than the former—more cerebral and abstract, and more of a test. But are jazz and weaving really less intellectual than oil painting? I doubt that anyone who has visited the breathtaking collection of baskets at the Yosemite Museum or seen the catalogue of the Elsie Allen Collection of baskets woven by the Pomo people would agree to the invidious comparisons. But supposing they are correct, why assume that the more cerebral has greater worth than the less cerebral?

Let me repeat that I do not minimize the significance of value considerations. Nor do I wish to underestimate the problems inherent in distinguishing assets from liabilities or in justifying such claims. My point is merely that a cultural-wealth framework does not require that these issues be settled in advance. In fact, one benefit of this perspective is that it allows submerged value issues to rise to the surface. Once they are made explicit, solutions to them can be worked out *within* the framework to which the concepts of cultural assets and liabilities belong.

As it happens, one major drawback of the reductive definition of cultural wealth now in place is that it makes the project of determining which portions of stock are valuable appear unnecessary. Obviously, a culture should transmit its wealth. Since "high" culture and the "higher" learning constitute that wealth, does it not follow that these are what should be passed along to future generations? The trouble with this reasoning is that the received definition of cultural wealth is selective. But then, in singling out only high culture and the higher learning as cultural wealth, we do not so much dispense with the evaluative work as conceal it. Deciding by fiat what the wealth consists in, we smuggle our value judgments into our definition of it perhaps without realizing we do so, and certainly without thinking enough about what else of value we may be excluding.

And now another puzzle arises. Poverty, slavery, terrorism, torture, domestic violence are not natural phenomena: They are learned, not innate. But then, according to the broad definition of culture, they are cultural practices. Must we therefore consider these a part of a culture's *wealth*? Not at all. *Representations of* immoral deeds and evil practices—whether historical, psychological, sociological, or philosophical studies; or fictional, artistic, photographic, or theatrical portrayals—can all belong to the wealth of cultures, although whether or not they do must be determined on a case-by-case basis. This wealth does not include the human atrocities themselves, however.

Think of the Nazi concentration camps and the uses to which they were put. They were creations of culture, not nature: of that there can be no doubt. Yet by no stretch of the imagination do they constitute part of the wealth of cultures. On the other hand, the artifacts of the camps, the photographs of victims and perpetrators, and the scale models in the Holocaust Memorial Museum in Washington, D.C., can certainly be said to increase cultural wealth. Providing the underpinnings for a coherent narrative about a culture's depravities, they enable visitors to connect to the victims of the story.

Think of the Rape of Nanking. Estimates are that between 260,000 and 350,000 noncombatants died at Nanking in 1937 at the hands of the Japanese (Chang, 1997). It is tempting to say that instead of adding to humankind's cultural riches, the German concentration camps and the actions of the Japanese soldiers so depleted its coffers as to put all of us in debt. But the metaphor of cultural wealth breaks down at just this juncture. Debts can be repaid, yet there is no way to undo what the Nazis and the Japanese did. Coffers can be filled again, but new cultural riches do not cancel out inhuman acts. True, cultural achievements such as the United Nations Declaration of Human Rights can be viewed as partial repayment of the debt incurred. Yet one takes the measure of a metaphor not just by the illumination it provides, but also by what it casts in shadow. My object in importing the language of assets and liabilities into the cultural domain is to make plain the vast dimensions of cultural abundance. The last thing I wish to do is hide human evil or trivialize its significance.

I have sometimes been asked why I place the metaphor of wealth in the very center of a culture-based approach to education. Doesn't the economic terminology debase my theory? Won't it encourage people to think of cultural objects in monetary terms? Indeed, by this action am I not implicitly subsuming culture under economics? These skeptical comments reflect a tendency to reduce the concept of wealth to one of its several forms. I, however, reject the equation of riches with economic value. "The price of wisdom is above rubies," says the Old Testament (Tripp, 1970, 1053:6). "The first wealth is health," wrote Ralph Waldo Emerson (Tripp, 1970, 411:5). Believing that there are different kinds of wealth and that the kind I am calling cultural is every bit as important to human societies as the economic kind, I intentionally employ language that challenges the false equation by placing the two kinds of riches on the same level.

Of course a cultural-wealth metaphor has its limitations, but so does every metaphor and analogy. In *The Selfish Gene*, evolutionary theorist Richard Dawkins (1976) introduced the concept of a meme—a unit of cultural transmission analogous to a gene. In many respects this biological analogy is peculiarly apt. For one thing, diversity and proliferation characterize nature as well as culture. For another, there is no denying the existence of either biological or cultural evolution—at least in the minimal sense of change over time. Perhaps most important, the biological analogy highlights the big and very controversial question that cultural-wealth imagery does not invite: Do cultural and biological evolution follow the same laws (Dennett, 1991, 1995)?

My cultural-wealth metaphor does, however, have advantages of its own. In particular, this imagery allows one to say that both assets *and* liabilities constitute a culture's stock from which source its cultural wealth is drawn. A culture's wealth, in other words, is only that portion of cultural stock that is deemed valuable. Arbitrarily designating "high" culture and the "higher" learning our only valuable stock, we make the process of forgetting the problem of what to pass down to our children that much easier. Define cultural wealth narrowly and the mandate to transmit the cultural heritage to the next generation is of course greatly simplified. Selection will still be necessary since even "high" culture is so abundant that one cannot map all of it onto any given person's curriculum. But the twin problems of cultural abundance and curricular selection will at least appear manageable. Granted, with a nonreductive definition of cultural wealth, one might still end up deciding to transmit only high culture. However, the choice would have been made in full recognition that only a single portion of wealth was being passed down.

One welcome consequence of a broad interpretation of a culture's stock is that it makes the question of why one portion is being transmitted and some other is not appear legitimate instead of laughable. At the curriculum conference on excellence, the speaker who was so loath to discuss the issue of abundance cited basket weaving as a good example of the kind of study that in her opinion was then threatening the quality of American education. I am not aware that anyone has ever proposed that basket weaving be incorporated into the school curriculum, but the audience's laughter left no doubt as to its estimate of the idea.

For reasons I have never fully understood, basket weaving has long been a staple of educational humor in the United States. I used to wonder why its very mention was considered funny and to harbor the suspicion that its association with societies presumed to be less "advanced" or "civilized" than our own—and, of course, its association with women—made it fair game. I now realize that jokes at its expense tap into the shared assumption that education's mandate to transmit our cultural heritage to the next generation amounts to a mandate to transmit "high" culture and the "higher" learning. Do I read too much into the speaker's modest attempt at humor? Isn't basket weaving an object of educational mirth because it is a trivial pursuit in contemporary society? Although she and most members of her audience seemed to view it in this light, something other than its presumed lack of importance was implicated in the joke. After all, if triviality were the issue, the speaker could have cited some of the trivial tracts and treatises, facts and opinions belonging to the "higher" learning. Basket weaving was amusing in a way these would not have been because it is not the kind of thing that people include in their conception of "high" culture. Reasonable men and women operate on the assumption that we should be passing our accumulated wealth down to the next generation. This is why they find the very idea of including basket weaving in the American curriculum so absurd.

The reduction of culture in general to "high" culture and the "higher" learning—in other words, to culture with a capital C—is so deeply ingrained in many people's consciousness that they do not notice the absurdity of a definition of culture that mistakes a part for the whole. It verges on the ridiculous that a nation which takes pride in being a literate culture and constantly worries that literacy rates may have declined considers the three Rs as tools for acquiring culture but not as items of cultural wealth in their own right. It is equally inconsistent to call the existence of moral codes one of the marks of civilization, yet define cultural wealth so that they do not belong to it. And it makes little sense that cultural products such as political practices, medical treatments, engineering skills—indeed the whole range of human occupations—are excluded from this category.

The problem with any reductive definition of cultural wealth is that every culture's stock is broadly based. No single type of thing can possibly exhaust its wealth because so many types constitute its stock. Were cultural wealth a purely theoretical construct having no practical application, an exclusionary rendering of it would be of little consequence. Education's mandate to transmit the cultural heritage anchors this concept in everyday affairs, however. After all, what is a culture's heritage if it is not its wealth? Of course, in the name of transmitting that heritage a culture may, in spite of its good intentions, hand down cultural liabilities to its young—for instance, the practices of child abuse or racism—as well as assets. Yet surely the object is to pass on to them whatever cultural stock is perceived to be of value. And just as certainly, insofar as cultural wealth is identified with "high" culture and the "higher" learning, a nation or society will be ignoring the greater part of its wealth.

Still and all, a nonreductive definition of cultural wealth appears to have one fatal flaw, namely that of assigning value to trivial pursuits. In actuality, however, a definition that is democratic in the sense of being broad enough to include the contributions of all members of society over the whole range of contexts no more settles the question of the relative value of the various items of cultural wealth than Smith's democratized definition of the wealth of nations prejudged the value of the various commodities. Thus, to include basket weaving in the category of cultural wealth is not for a moment to say that this activity belongs in the American school curriculum. To be sure, if it is counted part of cultural wealth, it might be difficult for educators to treat it quite so cavalierly as they often have. But I take this to be a point in favor of a broad definition of cultural wealth, for the triviality of basket weaving is by no means a self-evident truth.

Of all the trivial questions I have encountered while playing the game Trivial Pursuit, to me the most trivial is: Who was accompanying Patricia Hearst the day she was kidnapped? Yet as unimportant as this fact is to me, it cannot have been trivial to Stephen Weed, the person in question— or, presumably, to Patricia Hearst herself. When I visited Oxford, had I seen the round, broad-brimmed hat belonging to Cardinal Wolsey in its small glass case in the library of Christ Church, I doubt that I would have thought another thing about it. Yet one very interesting new area of scholarship, the "new historicism," takes as its point of departure this and sundry other items that to me appear so trivial as to have no redeeming value (Greenblatt, 1990). I realize how dangerous it is to generalize on the basis of but two examples. In the present instance, however, it seems fair to say that one person's trivial pursuit is another's vital occupation.

It is also fair to conclude that education as well as scholarship can turn seemingly trivial artifacts into objects of importance. As the cardinal's hat can point a Renaissance scholar to Catholic rituals and Reformation rhetoric, basket weaving can point students to the history of technology, cross-cultural differences in gender roles, a comparative study of food production and consumption, and the symbolic uses of design.

In excluding basket weaving and other apparently trivial pursuits *by definition* from the category of cultural wealth, we deny ourselves the opportunity to discover their educational possibilities. We also run the risk that the know-how will become extinct rather than something that someone might some day be able to adapt to new purposes. A reductive definition of cultural wealth does more damage than this, however. It is a dangerous policy because no single institution of a society is the conservator of a culture's whole wealth.

If one benefit of a cultural-wealth approach is that it encourages one to distinguish between cultural assets and liabilities, another is that it acknowledges the central role that institutions play in cultural preservation and transmission. In contrast, the biological imagery of meme theory conceals the societal aspect of these processes. Of course, for some purposes it may not matter that institutions have been dropped out of the picture. When the subject is education, however, we ignore institutions at our peril.

Suppose a portion of the whole were being squandered by one of the custodians; or, less melodramatically, that for reasons beyond anyone's control, its guardian could no longer preserve and nurture it. If the assets were not considered to belong to the culture's wealth, their loss would not even be noticed. If noticed, their disappearance would cause no alarm. On the other hand, if the items appeared on an inventory of cultural wealth, they would sooner or later be missed, whereupon decisions could be made about whether a new form of guardianship was required.

The supposition is not purely hypothetical. The guardianship of the old farmer's know-how was once a family matter; but, for complex economic, technological, and sociological reasons quite beyond the control of any one individual or family grouping, the self-appointed caretaker of this portion of our wealth is no longer able to carry out its responsibilities. That we are only dimly aware of this historic trend and quite unmoved by it is an alarming confirmation of the desperate need for a panoramic view of the contents of cultural wealth.

To cite another case in point, at the time I write it is no longer possible to ignore how violent America's youth—in particular its boys and young men—have become. Some have blamed the movement of women into the workforce for this condition. But almost no one who recognizes that the changes in home and family are irrevocable has thought to ask if these institutions have become ineffectual transmitters of the three Cs of care, concern, and connection. Since we do not count such virtues in our cultural wealth, it does not occur to most of us that home and family have traditionally been considered their custodians. Nor do we stop to think that if they are no longer being adequately conserved or successfully handed down, new guardians may have to be appointed.

PRESERVING THE STOCK; OR, THE FAILURES OF THE INVISIBLE HAND

"Why do you want to tear down a beautiful 19th-century house that's in very good condition?" the member of the Newton, Massachusetts, Historical Commission asked. "I bought the property to make money," replied the man who was seeking permission to demolish a Queen Anne–style landmark and erect four brand new colonials in its place. Visibly shaken by this threat to the city's cultural wealth and only too well aware of their inability to prevent its being carried out, the guardians of my town's riches gave the building a 6-month stay of execution (Cassidy, 1995).

"Come September," I said to a young man I know, "the house will be gone." "Why do you care?" he responded. "Why isn't a new house *better* than an old one?" The builder's son had asked the same question. Resenting the commissioners' quite evident disdain for his father's values, that passionate advocate had informed the government's representatives that his family had earned a reputation for building high-quality houses. Yes, they were going to tear down an old wreck. But in its place they intended to put up four dwellings of the finest workmanship.

Before the hearing it had seemed obvious to me that the old house should be preserved, yet when challenged I could think of no way to support my position other than to say that the doomed structure was both old and magnificent. "You can see from the one that's now under construction that the new houses will be very good-looking. Maybe not magnificent, but definitely nice, and far more energy-efficient," my devil's advocate insisted. His question did not cause me to change my opinion of the approaching demolition, but it made me wonder if the high assessment I was putting on the old house was as arbitrary and self-serving as the builder's low estimate seemed to be.

For some months I asked myself why I leaned toward the old. It was not mere reflex. I am no collector of antiques or student of the classics. Nor was it sheer romance. The moment the commissioners started discussing the old house's architectural fine points in loving detail, my mind wandered. Only when I thought in general terms about the preservation of a culture's stock and the transmission of its wealth was I able to explain to my own satisfaction why even four nice-looking new houses were no compensation for the destruction of the old.

Let me not exaggerate the dimensions of the cultural loss. The old house was one of several examples of its architectural style in my city, although its site—it stood with a small carriage house on a large lot on the crest of a hill—made it unique. Moreover, photographs do exist. Thus, if future generations want to know how the house and neighborhood once looked, they can find out.

On the other hand, there is no reason to expect the city's appointed guardians to succeed in protecting the still-surviving instances of the Queen Anne style, should their safety be threatened. And although visual representations of houses are also cultural assets, they do not convey the same sense of the past as do the houses themselves. One could walk around the old house as one could a piece of sculpture. One could touch the wood if one wanted, peer at decorations that had escaped photographers' lenses, and even inspect the way the building had been put together. If one was invited inside, one could also try to imagine how the original inhabitants had lived. From the house itself, in other words, one could gain an intimate three-dimensional feel for history.

I hasten to add that the validity of the argument for preserving the old house was by no means a foregone conclusion. If the building had been so unsound as to endanger neighboring structures or had become so contaminated by pollutants as to put the community's health at risk, its demolition might well have been justified. If its maintenance had entailed significant environmental losses or, perhaps, the annihilation of other equally valuable cultural assets, the drastic act might have been warranted. Nor were the reasons for maintaining the old house on the original site incontrovertible. To be sure, when structures—not rickety huts but beautiful, solid, historical buildings—are left standing, a neighborhood will constitute a kind of unplanned living museum. As neighborhoods change, however, it may be necessary to move an old house to a new location in order to preserve the culture's wealth. Or prudence might dictate that the house be placed in a specially constructed preserve: a well-planned living museum of 19th-century New England, for instance, or even a kind of "old-age home" for houses.

To say that the claims for preservation of an item of cultural wealth can sometimes be overridden by special circumstances is not, however, to say that excusing conditions existed in the case of this old house. The appearance on our street in mid-September of a carload of licensed demolition experts and a wrecker the size of a tyrannosaurus rex was due strictly to a capitalist's desire for profit. "Every individual is continually exerting himself to find out the most advantageous employment for whatever capital he can command. It is his own advantage, indeed, and not that of the society which he has in view," Adam Smith wrote in *The Wealth of Nations* (1776/1976, p. 475). In intending only his own gain and directing his industry to that end, the destroyer of the old house was the very model of Smith's good capitalist.

Although a self-interested individual "neither intends to promote the public interest, nor knows how much he is promoting it" said Smith, that person is likely to further the interest of society "more effectually than when he really intends to promote it" (1776/1976, pp. 477–478). This happy outcome is assured because one who intends nothing but his own private gain will be "led by an invisible hand to promote an end which was not part of his intention" (p. 477). Whether the builder's act of self-interest was metamorphosed into a contribution to the nation's *economic* welfare, I do not know. No sleight of hand, however, could transform the demolition into a contribution to this nation's *cultural* wealth.

Smith was not so naive as to think that all individuals act in their own best interests all the time. Indeed, he went so far as to say that to the extent that they do not, the public good will not be served. The builder, however, was not guilty of the misconduct that worried Smith: He was not squandering economic capital instead of accumulating it. His *mis*conduct was a direct result of what Smith considered *good* conduct. From the standpoint of cultural stock, the razing of the old house was a wastefully extravagant act. From the point of view of the builder's own economic gain, demolition was the prudent, the frugal, the right thing to do.

I do not want to paint too grim a picture of cultural loss. There are many wonderful instances of good conduct toward the past—some as prosaic as cookbooks, others as uncommon as the living museums at Williamsburg, Virginia, and Sturbridge, Massachusetts. I, for one, have come away from Old Sturbridge Village feeling a different person, so enriched was I by my new knowledge of the past, and even more so by my vicarious experience of the ways of living of an earlier time. And the *Boston Globe* has reported that at Williamsburg, where a program entitled "Enslaving Virginia" opened in 1999, "visitors—particularly children—often find themselves unexpectedly drawn into the plot. 'Peter, Peter,' cried 10-year-old J.D. Touchton as he scurried to one of the key slave characters in the unfolding skit. 'Be careful, be careful. The slave patrol is coming. They're coming'" (Koh, 1999, p. A3). In contrast to the information one gets from history books and lectures—themselves vehicles for preserving cultural assets—this "knowledge by acquaintance" engages the senses and emotions, thereby bringing intuition and empathy into play.

In books and lectures old practices and occupations are described and analyzed. At Williamsburg and Sturbridge Village old practices and occupations are reconstructed and reenacted. At the Hull House Labor Museum that Jane Addams created not long after the 1889 opening of her settlement house in Chicago, practitioners performed these activities themselves.

In *Twenty Years at Hull-House*, Addams told of seeing an old Italian woman sitting on the steps of a tenement. Holding up her spindle, the recent immigrant informed Addams that when she had spun enough yarn, she would knit a pair of stockings. "Could we not interest the young people working in the neighboring factories, in these older forms of industry, so that, through their own parents and grandparents, they would find a dramatic representation of the *inherited resources* of their daily occupation," Addams asked (1907/1990, p. 139; emphasis added). Her answer was to fit up a room at Hull House, the settlement house she and Ellen Gates Starr had established in Chicago in 1889, "to which we might invite those of our neighbors who were possessed of old crafts and who were eager to use them" (p. 139). There she arranged in historical sequence the different methods of spinning represented in the neighborhood and related them to the then-extant factory method, thus accomplishing her twofold aim of preserving cultural stock and, in the process, restoring the dignity of the uprooted older generation.

Early-music groups can be said to do for baroque compositions, instruments, and performance practices what the Hull House Labor Museum did for old European industries and what Sturbridge Village does for rural life in 18th-century New England. Using period violins and trumpets to perform well-known compositions, unearthing the forgotten scores of oft-performed composers, and resurrecting old composers themselves, these organizations make it their business to preserve cultural wealth. Music historians, in turn, preserve the wealth when they track down and compile once-popular compositions such as those written for the piano in 19th-century New Orleans. Folklorists preserve it when on tape or by dictation they capture songs and stories handed down from one generation to the next.

Museums and libraries, opera companies and ballet corps, recording companies and publishing houses, historical societies and book clubs: These and countless other institutional forms have been created to recover, protect, and nurture cultural assets. Some of the custodial arrangements serve simply as warehouses for keeping old stock. Others put tools, diaries, household goods, musical scores, and other artifacts on display. Some treat practices and artifacts alike as rusty relics. Transmitting as they preserve, others put the relics into a form in which they can be studied and understood. On occasion they even provide opportunities for something more.

The Hiroshima Peace Memorial Museum has two wings. In the east building facts are displayed about Hiroshima both before and after August 6, 1945, the day an atomic bomb was dropped on the city. The west building contains the possessions of people who died in the bombing. "It is our hope," says the museum pamphlet, "that through these materials visitors to this museum will reflect on the importance of abolishing nuclear weapons and realizing lasting world peace, the earnest wish of Hiroshima."

The assumption that underlies the Holocaust Memorial Museum is also very simple: When we suppress memory of the Holocaust, we promote the emergence of future holocausts. Hoping to kindle remembrance, the museum gives each visitor the identity card of a concentration camp victim or survivor. You and your "passport companion" then embark on a journey during which you are surrounded by artifacts retrieved from Auschwitz and other sites and by photograph upon photograph of the victims and survivors, their families and friends.

In addition to institutions such as museums that have been specifically designed to protect and preserve the wealth, ones such as school, home, church, neighborhood, and workplace do so in the course of transmitting it to the next generation. Preservation and transmission may be theoretically distinct processes—the one directed to the protection of assets for the next generation and the other to handing the stock over, passing it down to them—yet these two functions are often so intimately connected in practical life as to be virtually indistinguishable. Keep a set of documents in an archive long enough for the next generation to take physical possession of it and it will, in effect, have been transmitted to them. Teach your skills to your sons and daughters and your know-how will be preserved.

At one point in his breathtaking history of the last 13,000 years, physiologist Jared Diamond takes the plant's point of view. "Like all animal species (including humans)," he says, "plants must spread their offspring to areas where they can thrive and pass on their parents' genes" (1999, p. 115). Diamond does not, of course, attribute to them a conscious intent to propagate. Rather, the evolutionary analysis he adopts portrays the behavior of plants *as if* it were goal-directed. Meme theorists, in turn, look at cultural transmission through the eyes of the meme and portray the behavior of even such minute memes as the first four notes of Beethoven's Fifth Symphony as if it were goal-directed. "The haven all memes depend on reaching is the human mind," says philosopher Daniel Dennett (1995, p. 365), and there is "a considerable competition among memes for entry into as many minds as possible" (p. 349).

Perhaps the behavior of the custodians of our culture's wealth can also be illuminated by evolutionary theory. I do not want to rule out the possibility. But so far as I am able to determine, the behavior of the custodians of our stock does not in all cases mimic that of one who consciously intends to preserve the wealth. On the contrary, despite the number and variety of custodians, our assets are not secure.

Smith wrote, "It can seldom happen that the circumstances of a great nation can be much affected either by the prodigality or misconduct of individuals; the profusion or imprudence of some, being always more than compensated by the frugality and good conduct of others" (1776/1976, p. 362). A nation's cultural wealth may not be threatened by the squandering of a few individuals if their imprudence is compensated for by the frugality of the majority. But the prospect of such compensation is not warranted when people do not know what cultural assets they possess and, in any case, exhibit a devil-may-care attitude toward that inheritance.

John Stuart Mill, the British philosopher whose own 1848 treatise on economics became a classic in the field, believed that people by nature act so as to maximize their own pleasure or happiness. Where Smith seemed to think that capitalism was innate, Mill took men and women, one and all, to be hedonists by birth. Yet Mill was also the person who said that every individual should act so as to maximize the happiness of the greatest number. Having no faith in miracles and finding no evidence whatsoever that an invisible hand—or, for that matter, evolutionary processes—would make things right, he looked to education to bring private pleasure into line with the public good. Education and opinion, he wrote in *Utilitarianism*, should so use their power over human character "as to establish in the mind of each individual an indissoluble association between his own happiness and the good of the whole" (Mill, 1863/1962, p. 269). Mill made it clear, however, that it was not enough simply to rule out the possibility in people's minds of happiness to oneself being consistent with conduct opposed to the general good. Education and opinion should also make sure that "a direct impulse to promote the general good may be in every individual one of the habitual motives of action, and the sentiments connected therewith may fill a large and prominent place in every human being's sentient existence" (p. 269).

Discovering no signs of an invisible hand that guides private intention, be it for profit or pleasure, I in turn look to education and opinion to put a halt to our collective squandering. Like Mill and many others, I know that education does not take place only in schools. Wherever it is housed, however, education can and should so employ its power as to establish in girls and boys, men and women, builders and buyers, citizens and governors a direct impulse to preserve the wealth of cultures, along with the sentiments connected therewith.

TRANSMITTING THE LEGACY;
OR, CULTURAL LOSS AND RENEWAL

The summer I turned 14 I received just such an education at Camp Woodland in Phoenicia, New York. "Do you mean to tell me that the whole camp swims in that little pool?" my horrified mother asked on Visiting Day. "Wouldn't you prefer a camp with a lake? What do you do all day?" One of the things we did was participate in what I have since discovered was a unique project of "living conservation."[1]

Starting in 1939 the camp, under the leadership of Norman Studer, undertook to preserve and act as a custodian of the heritage of a fairly large region of the Catskill Mountains. For generations Catskill families had passed down their mores to their children. But now the encroachments of the city and the dislocations caused by the building of a dam were putting the area's culture at risk. Having no faith that an invisible hand would protect the wealth, Studer proposed that the camp step into the breach. To this end, campers and counselors alike traveled through the Phoenicia area taking down oral histories, collecting artifacts, and recording songs and ballads—first strictly in notation and later on tape. Ox yokes, bed warmers, old pieces of wooden water pipe, and a wood "splitter" with an ad-

---

[1]Papers, photographs, reel-to-reel tapes, and old work implements that document this project in particular, and Camp Woodland's history and accomplishments more generally, are housed in the Norman Studer Archives at the M. E. Grenander Department of Special Collections and Archives, New Library Building, State University of New York, Albany, New York 12222.

justable knife were then placed in the camp's makeshift museum and the entire camp learned to sing George Edwards's "I Walk the Road Again."

Reflecting on that amazing camp experience, I now see that in the very processes of recovery and preservation, the cultural wealth of the Catskills was itself affected. The act of removing an artifact from its cultural nexus, be it to a children's camp or a world-renowned art institute, always entails a loss of meaning.

Dewey wrote in *Art as Experience*:

> Domestic utensils, furnishings of tent and house, rugs, mats, jars, pots, bows, spears, were wrought with such delighted care that today we hunt them out and give them places of honor in our art museums. Yet in their own time and place, such things were enhancements of the processes of everyday life. Instead of being elevated to a niche apart, they belong to display of prowess, the manifestation of group and clan membership, worship of gods, feasting and fasting, fighting, hunting, and all the rhythmic crises that punctuate the stream of living. (1934, p. 6)

In a sense, then, unless it be a tool of torture that is best taken out of circulation, placing a material object in a showroom where it is no longer called upon to perform the function for which it was designed subtracts from its value. As for folk songs, even the best transcriber into standardized notation had to tailor and trim George Edwards's inimitable renditions.

Yet it is not only deliberate, self-conscious preservers and collectors of cultural wealth such as Camp Woodland and the Metropolitan Museum of Art that alter the heritage. As laments over the fate of George Balanchine's ballets demonstrate, cultural loss does not occur only when ethnomusicologist meets folksinger.

Ten years before Balanchine died in 1983, he began filming his ballets for archival purposes. Yet although the act reveals that he was thinking of his works as artifacts to be preserved for posterity, he also wanted to hand them down as a living legacy: "People dance while I'm here, they dance a certain way. When I'm gone, they will continue dancing, but somebody will rehearse them different and it will all be a little different, with different approach, different intensity. So a few years go by and I won't be here. Will be my ballets, but will look different" (Croce, 1993, p. 99).

Balanchine not only established a school in which to train dancers to his ideal, he named his successor. Still, just 10 years after his death, a critic described the "catastrophically swift decline" of Balanchine's repertory. The master had forecast that his work would live in some recognizable living form until the first decade of the 21st century. His disciple could see that its ruin was "all but complete" as of June 1993. The ballets, she said, have not suffered the deterioration that is to be expected over time. Rather, they "have had their hearts torn out." They live on "not as ballets that have changed but as empty demonstrations of formerly meaningful spectacles" (Croce, 1993, p. 100).

The process of change that the critic said was built into the art of ballet is a given for any practice. Tastes change, values change, behavioral patterns change; new technologies are introduced and new worldviews yield new ways of interpreting even the most ordinary experience. With everything in flux, it would be an unbending art indeed—or sport, trade, profession, institution, rite, ritual, theory, doctrine, or ideology, for that matter—that did not respond in kind. Yet change need not spell decay. Wine improves with age, and so do many people. Even in Balanchine's case, change and deterioration are not synonymous: Although the technique in his ballets changed considerably from the 1950s to the 1970s, his final decade of creativity was marked by "burst upon burst of glory" (Croce, 1993, p. 99).

Only when there is perfection does change have to be for the worse, for in that case it will necessarily represent a falling away from the ideal. Whether or not one judges Balanchine's works to have achieved perfection, his case is instructive. Teaching that change is unavoidable when a practice is handed down to the next generation, it raises the question of whether people might not legitimately disagree about how well or badly a cultural practice has survived the ravages of time. Summoning up the specter of deterioration, it also brings to the surface the extraordinarily difficult problem of how much modification some cultural asset can undergo before it forfeits the old label.

This last is a version of the tantalizing philosophical problem of what entitles us to attribute identity to something that changes over time. What justifies my calling the young girl I see in a photograph and my 98-year-old aunt the same person when they are in almost every respect so utterly different? Given all the renovations it has undergone over the years, what allows me to call an old house the same one that a sea captain built in 1885? Indeed, what entitles me to say that "I Walk the Road Again," when sung lustily to guitar or piano accompaniment, is the selfsame song that George Edwards half sang, half spoke, in a twang that we campers could only approximate? What enables Americans to call their Constitution, with all its amendments and its 200-plus-year history of reinterpretation, the selfsame document that the founders signed in 1789?

I once would have judged the dance reviewer right to say that a given practice—or institution, theory, doctrine, for that matter—cannot survive having its heart torn out. But advances in medical technology now cast doubt on even this conclusion. Besides, what the reviewer did not say is that there can be legitimate disagreement about what *constitutes* the meta-phorical heart of something that, literally speaking, does not possess this organ. Is style the heart of the matter in Balanchine's case, as she implied? Might not the dancers who came to the defense of Balanchine's designated successor name some other attribute?

Certainly, the heirs to other inheritances have disagreed about the heart of the matter. In the case of Marx, disciples have argued about whether the core or essence of his thought is his historical materialism, his economic analysis, or his concepts of class conflict and consciousness. In Freud's case, they have differed about whether it is his theory of the unconscious, his tripartite analysis of personality, or the techniques of psychoanalysis. Sects have been founded on the various judgments of what the heart of Marx's, Freud's, and, of course, Jesus' teachings "really" is. And in these cases, as in Balanchine's, I for one would question whether a given practice or a belief system even *has* a heart, in the sense of one or a small set of properties without which it cannot be said to exist.

A purist might call it an empty exercise to inquire into the wealth of cultures before the philosophical problem of identity over time is solved. I, however, consider the advice to postpone investigation misguided. En-during philosophical problems are not like crossword puzzles: They do not have a single right answer that, when discovered, is self-evident to all. If a "solution" suddenly became available, it would itself be an object of le-gitimate disagreement. But then, in the interests of consistency, our purist would still advise against our proceeding with this inquiry.

Actually, where cultural wealth is concerned, the purist's advice makes little sense in any case. If by some miracle the problem of identity over time were solved to everyone's satisfaction, the question of which items of cul-tural stock should be passed down to the next generation as living lega-cies would remain. So would the question of what to do about those ideas and practices that for one reason or another become rigidified in the pro-cess of transmission.

"Mr. B. did not want the company to become a museum piece," said a ballerina who disputed the reviewer's judgment (Temin, 1993). As those who worry about the average age of symphony orchestra audiences and the dwindling attendance at Sturbridge Village realize full well, an asset can also become irrelevant. Practices, theories, and the rest were developed in the first place in relation to deeply felt human interests and purposes. When these change—and they do over time—the practices themselves may become detached from their human and social moorings. Even if they live up to the standards imposed on them by their creators, they may be re-garded as relics of a past age. The interests and purposes of the next gen-eration do not have to change, however, for old practices to be superseded.

When knowledge and technology change, they can so alter a society's estimate of a practice's effectiveness as to lead to its abandonment.

At what point should the bequeathers or the bequeathed attempt to restore an item of cultural stock to its original state? When should they give up their struggles, and what should they do then? A solution to the problem of identity over time sheds little light on questions of cultural forgetting and loss. The answers to these depend on how highly the older generation values a given parcel of stock, on that group's perceptions of the next generation's needs, and on its estimates of how well the asset will survive the ravages of time. The answer depends also on that generation's own perceptions and wishes, for they themselves are active participants in the process of cultural transmission.

Lest we forget, change can mean renewal as well as deterioration; it can represent gain rather than loss. German sociologist Karl Mannheim once pointed out that because cultural creation and cultural accumulation are not accomplished by the same individuals, "our culture is developed by individuals who come into contact anew with the accumulated heritage. In the nature of our psychical make-up, a fresh contact (meeting something anew) always means a changed relationship of distance from the object and a novel approach in assimilating, using, and developing the proffered material" (1952, p. 293). Mannheim was keenly aware that "the continuous emergence of new human beings certainly results in some loss of accumulated cultural possessions," yet he maintained that this fact of social life has its compensations. The continuous emergence of new human beings, he said, "makes a fresh selection possible when it becomes necessary; it facilitates reevaluation of our inventory and teaches us both to forget that which is no longer useful and to covet that which has yet to be won" (p. 294). Implying that the heritage would stagnate in a world in which transmission of the cultural legacy to a new generation was unnecessary, he concluded that our real world is saved from this fate because new generations always offer the potential for growth and development.

The potential is certainly there. New generations produce new ideas, new art, new music, new patterns of behavior; they adapt old items of wealth to new interests and purposes; and along the way they discard some of what their predecessors treasured. One good example is the reevaluation of received theories and narratives provided by the new scholarship on women and minorities. This work also replenishes the wealth by reclaiming ideas and practices and experiences that have long been excluded from the legacy.

Whether Mannheim's overall optimism is justified, however—in other words, whether the new generation's creation of brand-new stock and its adaptations of old stock will cancel out a culture's losses over time—I do not know. I do not think anyone does, for the potential to turn assets into liabilities is also there. Nor do I know an easy solution to the very real problem of how a culture should divide its resources between the preservation of old stock and the creation of new. While lamenting yet one more revival of *The Sound of Music*, a music critic wrote, "Revivals deserve a place on the Great White Way, but the danger of old works pushing out new ones remains, and young creators are languishing" (Tommassini, 1998, p. 25). On the other hand, economist Amartya Sen has said:

> Lost traditions may be greatly missed. The demise of old ways of living can cause anguish, and a deep sense of loss. It is a little like the extinction of older species of animals. The elimination of old species in favor of "fitter" species that are "better" able to cope and multiply can be a source of regret, and the fact that the new species are "better" in the Darwinian system of comparison need not be seen as consolation enough. (1999, p. 241)

What I do know and what I hope is clear by now is that a culture's stock—and by extension its wealth—is both superabundant and in a state of perpetual fluidity. "Isn't one of the hallmarks of cultural evolution and transmission the extraordinarily high rate of mutation and recombination? We seldom pass on a meme unaltered," commented Dennett (1995, p. 355). With each portion of the stock subject to change, with some items no longer as valuable as they once were, with other items flourishing, with some stock taking on new meanings, and with new stock constantly emerging—being found or created or invented—while old stock is forgotten, the whole of a culture's stock is itself in flux.

CHAPTER 2

Multiple Educational Agency

EDUCATION AND SCHOOLING; OR, ANOTHER FALSE EQUATION

My friend describes to me her inner dialogues with the mother whose teachings she would momentarily like to forget. I tell her that scarcely a day passes when I do not attribute some feeling, attitude, or behavior of mine to the lessons of one or the other of my parents. She and I talk about the films and plays we have seen that portray educational transactions between mother and daughter, father and son, sister and brother, coach and athlete, domestic servant and child. And on my way home I am puzzled.

Malcolm X told college audiences: "I finished the eight grade in Mason, Michigan. My high school was the black ghetto of Roxbury, Massachusetts. My college was in the streets of Harlem, and my master's was taken in prison" (1966, p. 282). It is common knowledge that education is everywhere. No one raises an eyebrow when religious leaders present themselves as educators, museums house education departments, television networks label some programs "educational." No one thinks that school and university teachers are the only educators in our midst. On the other hand, the founder of San Francisco's "hands-on" science museum, the Exploratorium, was rebuffed when he asked the state of California to make his institution an official part of its educational system (Hein, 1990). I say that I am a philosopher of education and someone invariably wants to know if I write about elementary, secondary, or higher education—a three-part distinction pertaining strictly to schools. You open a newspaper or magazine to its education section expecting to read about schools and universities. The government appoints a new commissioner of education and we all assume that his or her domain is the nation's schools. A scholar says that educational levels have risen in the United States when what he means is that there has been an increase in years of schooling (Putnam, 2000).

In *Deschooling Society*, Ivan Illich explained how the reduction of education to one of its many forms—schooling—had gained currency. Drawing an analogy between school and church, he pointed out that both institutions divide social reality into two realms. As the one distinguishes between the sacred and the profane, the other separates the educational from the noneducational. As the church names itself the sole guardian of the sacred, school appoints itself keeper of the educational. With professions and even time spans labeled "academic," Illich said, the power of school "to divide social reality has no boundaries: education becomes unworldly and the world becomes noneducational" (1972, p. 35).

It was not always this way. The family was the main agency of education in the forming of U.S. society, and whatever it did not accomplish, the local community and the church undertook (Bailyn, 1960). Besides parents and young children, the extended colonial family typically consisted of a single household that included grown children, nieces and nephews, cousins, and, except in the case of the very poor, a range of servants. This shaped the attitudes, patterns of behavior, manners, and morals of all the young in its care and, in addition, gave instruction in the agricultural or trade skills they would need as adults. The external community then reinforced the instruction young people received at home while introducing them to the outside world and, in particular, to governmentally imposed discipline. Finally, the church gave formal instruction in Christian doctrine while initiating children into the conceptual framework and the imagery underlying the culture's way of understanding and interpreting human existence.

Schools existed in the United States in the early colonial period, but they played a relatively small role. Indeed, although Thomas Jefferson was a firm advocate of schooling, he never thought of school as the chief educational influence on the young (Cremin, 1965). In Jefferson's eyes, the press and participation in politics were the main educational agencies. Even when a system of free, universal, public schooling was under construction in the mid-19th century, most people took school to be a minor part of education. The generation that instituted "the common school" is also the one that established public libraries, lyceums, mechanics' institutes, agricultural societies, penny newspapers. And the next generation introduced still more agencies, among them the settlement house.

One of the first projects undertaken at Hull House was a reading club for young women. Soon thereafter a kindergarten was established and along with it a story-telling club for boys. Before long there were evening lectures on every conceivable subject: art classes for young and old; a music school complete with chorus, instrumental instruction, lessons in composition, and efforts at recovering the folk songs of immigrant groups living in the neighborhood; theater productions galore in many different languages; wood and metal shops and an apprentice course in bookbindery that emphasized design, workmanship, and beauty; continuous instruction in sewing, millinery, embroidery, dressmaking, and—lo and behold— basket weaving.

Not all the education at Hull House was as formal as this list or a schedule of weekly events might suggest. With its open-door policy, the walls covered with reproductions of famous works of art, a lending library of pictures, and immigrant groups celebrating their holidays and dramatizing the legends of their heritages, Hull House self-consciously strove to be a veritable educational community. That fateful day when Jane Addams saw the old woman holding up her spindle, she had just been thinking, "perhaps the power to see life as a whole, is more needed in the immigrant quarter of a large city than anywhere else" (1907/1990, p. 139). Addams conceived of the Labor Museum as a way to "build a bridge between European and American experiences in such wise as to give them both more meaning and a sense of relation" (p. 139) and to "lay a foundation for reverence of the past which Goethe declares to be the basis of all sound progress" (p. 139).

Try now to imagine Adam Smith proposing his broad definition of the wealth of nations and at the same time giving tacit consent to the old mercantile system. The discrepancy between the traditional ways of thinking and acting and his new, enlarged vision of a nation's wealth would have been painfully apparent. A similarly jarring experience is in store for those who adopt a broad definition of cultural wealth while leaving intact the present, narrow conception of education as schooling. Granted, from a strictly logical point of view, a democratized concept of cultural wealth does not require an equally broad conception of educational agency. Prudence dictates, however, that the popular equation of education and schooling be scrapped.

Equate education with schooling and, as in the case of the reduction of cultural wealth to high culture and the higher learning, it is all too easy to forget about vast quantities of our culture's assets. When school is considered to be "the" agent of education and is granted a monopoly over the whole of educational agency, it is only natural to see it as the one true or legitimate transmitter of the heritage. The trouble is that although the assets in school's custody might then be assured safe passage, the wealth in the keep of other custodians—for instance, the old farmer's know-how or an immigrant's arts and crafts—will not be secure. In addition to the potential loss to posterity of those portions of the wealth in the keep of custodians other than school, the false equation masks the fact that a great many of our culture's guardians pass down liabilities as well as assets to the next generation. As if this were not reason enough to expand our concept of educational agency, a reductive definition of education all but precludes cooperation among the keepers of the heritage. If family, local communities, the media, churches, museums, and the rest are not even perceived to be educational agents, they will scarcely be thought of as bona fide transmitters of the wealth.

A broad definition of cultural wealth is well served by a broad conception of educational agency, one that encompasses the whole range of custodians of our culture's stock. However, a return to the early colonial period's triumvirate of family, church, and community is out of the question. We could not go back if we tried, for the world has changed too much. It is not just that a public school system now exists, although that is no small matter. Family, local community, and church have all been transformed. With the roles of Christian and citizen closely linked in colonial days, it was a relatively straightforward matter for organized religion to initiate children into the ethos and loyalties of state and society. Today, religion is segmented. Besides, with the secular and religious spheres—Illich's sacred and profane—now more sharply differentiated, churches cannot possibly fulfill that earlier educational function. Indeed, whereas organized religion was once both a unified and a unifying educational agent, it is now a fragmented and, all too frequently, a fragmenting one.

The local community is no longer able to do its earlier job either. When family and local community were so well integrated that children scarcely knew where home left off and neighborhood began, it was only natural for the one to reinforce the other's teachings. The urbanization and industrialization of the United States in tandem with a highly mobile and changing population conspired to pull family and community apart, however, and eventually to turn vast numbers of local communities into sites of poverty, disease, and shattered human relationships. One task the first settlement houses set themselves was the regeneration of the then-disintegrating neighborhoods into the close-knit, social, supportive educational environments they presumably had once been. Reading Addams's descriptions of the myriad activities of Hull House in its prime, one can only regret that they did not attain their goal. Pondering the drugs, the violence, the poverty, and the homelessness in local communities today, I am reminded how easy it is for even so powerful an educative agency as the local community once was to become miseducative by default.

It is fair to say that the local community is no longer able to reinforce and enlarge upon the education that used to be provided by the family, and it is also true that the family is no longer equipped to do the educational tasks it once undertook. In fact, the family has undergone three major changes that have affected the way it functions as an educational agent.

Historians tell us that the Puritans of Massachusetts and Connecticut deliberately transferred "the maimed functions of the family" to schools, thereby enlarging school's purpose beyond vocationalism "toward vaguer but more basic cultural goals" (Bailyn, 1960, p. 27). A second major change in "the" family was wrought by the Industrial Revolution. In a speech he delivered in Chicago in 1899, Dewey pointed out that the manufacturing processes that until recently had been done at home with children's participation had many educational benefits. Among other virtues, industry, responsibility, imagination, perseverance, and powers of observation were all learned this way. With the flight of work into factories, children are no longer acquiring these virtues, he warned. His solution? Put into school the kind of work that before the advent of the factory system was done by the family at home. Do so not for vocational purposes but to prevent those traits and dispositions from becoming extinct (Dewey, 1900/1956). In other words, transfer custody of this portion of cultural wealth from home to school so that it will continue to be handed down to future generations as a living legacy.

As women entered the workforce and as family structures changed radically in the last decades of the 20th century, a third transformation occurred, and once again some of the family's old educational functions were maimed. How else is one to explain the arrival in schools of children who had never used a fork or spoon? Why else did an acquaintance of mine recently speak with something akin to despair about the teenage girls in her community who are in the process of becoming lost souls? And why is the daily news filled with reports of boys of all ages running wild?

The unique pattern of educational agency that characterized an earlier historical period cannot be recovered, but this does not justify our giving school a monopoly over education. A broad conception of culture and cultural wealth demands a conception of educational agency both inclusive and flexible enough to include the full range of assets and of their custodians. Actually, it demands more than this, for it requires a concept of educational agency that will cover the custodians of the full range of *both* our assets *and* our liabilities. For where a culture's stock is concerned, education has a twofold task. Even as it seeks to transmit the wealth to the next generation, it must avoid handing down the liabilities it has also amassed.

DECENTRALIZED EDUCATIONAL AGENCY; OR, INSTITUTIONS AS EDUCATORS

Once when I was standing on line to board a plane headed for a midwestern city, I observed a wheelchair-bound young woman cheerfully discussing the weather in Cincinnati with a companion. The process of making my way to my seat in the very back of the plane was so fraught with discomfort that I gave that tableau no more thought—that is, until I looked up and saw what I will not soon forget. There the woman was—her wheelchair replaced by a walker on which she was leaning for dear life and her chatty companion replaced by a flight attendant who, inching backward and extending her arms as one does to a toddler, was urging the woman on. "They'll seat her in the first row," I told myself. "Well, the next row, then." But with each desperate step of the woman's I was proven wrong. I would gladly have given up my own seat, but what earthly use to her was 44F? So I watched that cruel walk down the aisle—everyone watched it—until she was safely deposited in her designated seat.

In *The Schoolhome* (Martin, 1992) I called home and school partners in the education of this or any nation's young. What I did not say enough about is that these are but two of society's educational agents. Church, neighborhood, police and fire departments, museums, historical societies, libraries, and archives; zoos, parks, playgrounds, aquariums, and arboretums; symphony orchestras, record clubs, recording companies, ballet troops, and opera houses; banks, businesses, and the stock market; newspapers, magazines, book clubs, bookstores, publishing houses; sports organizations, billboards, government agencies, the military establishment, nonprofit organizations, and environmental groups; TV, the Internet, and the media in all its multitudinous forms: These, the airline I traveled, and the myriad other institutions of society educate young and old.

In thinking about the multiplicity of educational agency, I am reminded of the French philosopher Michel Foucault's analysis of power. Foucault pointed out that we tend to imagine power as centralized: as coming from above and as being located in the hands of a sovereign. In fact, he said, power operates in all the nooks and crannies of society and gains "access to individuals themselves, to their bodies, their gestures, their daily actions" (1980, pp. 151–152). According to this view, power is located in schools, prisons, the confessional; in the psychiatric profession's diagnostic categories of mental illness, the medical profession's standards of obesity, a corporation's decision to play music while a caller is on hold, a magazine's tips on dieting, a department store's display of cosmetics.

Once the concept of power is decentralized, the list of its sites and sources becomes endless. When the equation between education and schooling is rejected and education is in its turn decentralized, so is the list of educational agents. Foucault did not deny that the state is important. He simply wanted the analysis of power to extend beyond it. And, as one interpreter has put it, he wanted it to begin "from the ground up, at the level of tiny local events" (Hacking, 1986, p. 28). In like-minded fashion, I acknowledge school's importance. But the analysis of educational agency needs to go beyond school. It also needs to recognize that educational agency can be seen at work from the ground up. Where, for example, does the subliminal message that war is natural whereas peace is hopelessly unrealistic come from? The sandbox, the playground, movies, television, electronic games all preserve and transmit cultural stock.

One of the worst by-products of a centralized conception of educational agency is that no unacknowledged educational agent can, in good logic, be charged with *mis*educating the populace. Yet in daily bombarding young people with unwholesome, antisocial models of living and in making these appear fatally attractive, the print and electronic media are guilty of doing precisely this. And the media do not act alone. In demonstrating its callousness toward that young woman's plight, in showing no shame or guilt about unnecessarily causing her excruciating pain, in exposing her to the pity—and in some cases, I fear, the contempt—of strangers, that airline was transmitting negative attitudes about people with disabilities to young and old alike.

Rousseau once said that education comes to us "from nature or from men or from things" (1762/1979, p. 38). Two centuries later Illich called things, models, peers, and elders the resources a child needs for "real learning" (1972, p. 109). I do not want to deny that learning derives from people and things, but neither do I wish to oversimplify educational agency. In relation to the preservation and transmission of cultural stock, there is a world of difference between a Mayan vase situated in its original burial site and that same object on display in a museum gallery, a world of difference between a mother singing the Brahms lullaby to a cradled infant and the same song sung as an encore on a concert stage.

In real life, one does not encounter things and people in the abstract "as such." To be sure, more or less by definition museums detach artifacts from their original social and cultural contexts. Public concert halls do the same for music. But although at first glance these settings may appear to be perfectly neutral, institutions such as the Boston Symphony Orchestra, the New York Public Library, the Museum of Modern Art merely substitute one social and ideological framework for another. Just think of the formal attire worn by symphony orchestra players. Just think about the location of the conductor, the huge divide between performers and audience, the unwritten rules governing applause. No, people and things are invariably embedded in some sociocultural context. And to make matters more complicated still, they display a maddening tendency to change contexts with abandon.

Acknowledging the contextual dimension of education, a cultural-wealth perspective designates the various institutions that transmit the culture's stock, rather than people and things, as educational agents. This approach interprets the category of "institution" very broadly so as to include associations, groups, cultural settings, and the like. Still, a skeptic may wonder whether institutions possess the requisite characteristics of educators (cf. Peters, 1967, 1972). He or she may deny that the subliminal messages they send add up to education. Isn't education a deliberate activity that aims at the acquisition of knowledge and understanding? Doesn't it presuppose voluntariness on the learner's part and intention on the educator's part?

Definitions abound that reduce education to a purely rational process whose participants always know what they are doing, do whatever they do voluntarily, and invariably act with conscious intent. Regrettably, such formulas play fast and loose with the facts. So much for the likes and dislikes, attitudes and values that are unconsciously picked up during formal spelling and geography lessons—what Dewey termed "collateral learning" (1938/1963, p. 48). So much for what the radical school reformers of the 1970s identified as a hidden curriculum of schooling in obedience and conformity. So much for society's dubious and presumably unintended practice of passing down to the next generation not only its accumulated wealth but also its accumulated liabilities.

Would that TV networks saw themselves as engaged in educating the public! Would that the advertising industry and mass-market publishers aimed at the transmission of knowledge and understanding! Would that the major airlines did so, too! Definitions that tightly bind education to intentions, values, consciousness, and rationality allow one the satisfaction of withholding the label "educator" from, for instance, the manufacturer of a computer game whose aim is an escalating body count. But like it or not, that company is sending messages about the acceptability of violence and the cheapness of life. Like it or not, TV talk shows whose producers say their job is to provide entertainment transmit values, attitudes, and information. Whether these amount to cultural assets or liabilities I leave an open question. But like it or not, the zoo accused by a reader of my local newspaper of miseducating children is handing down misleading messages to both children and adults about the characteristics of the animals in its keep (Yanne, 1997). Like it or not, the airline that flew us to Cincinnati was passing along cultural prejudices toward people with disabilities.

Rejecting analyses that give pride of place to intention, Foucault urged that the analysis of power "should not concern itself with power at the level of conscious intention or decision" (1979, p. 97). What is needed, he said, "is a study of power in its external visage, at the point where it is in direct and immediate relationship with that which we can provisionally call its object, its target, its field of application, there—that is to say—where it installs itself and produces its real effects" (p. 97).

Given the vast extent of our cultural stock, the incredible number of guardians thereof, and the very real danger that the United States is blithely transmitting its liabilities to the next generation, it is an equally great mistake to build intentionality and voluntariness into the very concept of educational agency. True, if a society's educational agents are to act responsibly and be held accountable for whatever miseducation they promote, it is imperative that they admit to being educators. If we do not wish to bankrupt our young by passing down our culture's liabilities rather than its assets, it is crucial that the whole range of education's agents transmit what is worthwhile. But these are goals that our culture needs to strive for. To insist that an institution must already see itself as a teacher or educator or that its learners must even now exhibit willingness or voluntariness is to turn our backs on the world.

To reduce education to the getting of knowledge and understanding is also to flaunt the facts. In the United States children do badly on geography tests: Press and public condemn the nation's schools. Seventeen-year-olds cannot come up with the dates of the Civil War or the name of the author of *Leaves of Grass*: The experts consider this sufficient reason to overhaul the entire system. Those same youngsters run drugs, vandalize neighborhoods, kill their peers—and no one blames their education.

What accounts for the wildly divergent responses to the two situations? It is as if an invisible hand bent on subverting the common good first dispatched all of education's agents except school and then went on to create the illusion that education consists simply in the transmission of knowledge.

Remarking some years ago that even if music is not knowledge, it can still be taught, the philosopher William Frankena pointed out that in discussions of education, theories of knowledge are relevant but they are never in themselves decisive (Frankena, 1970). If music is not knowledge, it can nevertheless qualify for inclusion in a school curriculum. If how to pickpocket or swindle constitutes a kind of knowledge, curriculum space is not therefore guaranteed it.

Why over the years has Frankena's warning gone unheeded? Why is curriculum regularly reduced to a mere shadow of itself? Indeed, why is the process of becoming educated reduced to one of its myriad aspects? No member of the new generation is able at birth to be kind to others or to withstand peer pressure. No one at birth is able to take pride in positive achievement or feel ashamed of wrongdoing. No person comes into this world with the skills needed to resolve conflicts nonviolently or the desire to take other people's needs and points of view into account. Nor do these traits and dispositions—or, for that matter, the traits of honesty, courage, a sense of justice, a heartfelt concern for the future of the earth, a tolerance of different opinions and lifestyles, the desire to make the world a better place for one's children—emerge full blown as a person matures. On the contrary, to be human is to acquire all these through education, or not at all. Nevertheless, by assuming without arguing the case that knowledge is the only cultural asset worth bequeathing to the next generation, we reduce the process of educating to the dispensing of knowledge and equate its reciprocal—becoming educated—with the getting of knowledge.

Even as I was writing these paragraphs, a young man told me that he agreed wholeheartedly with me about the importance of transmitting the three Cs of care, concern, and connection to the next generation. He then added that anyone who wants school to teach these virtues will have to broaden the definition of knowledge. When I protested that no matter how broadly you define knowledge, care, concern, and connection are not reducible to such, he responded: "What is not knowledge cannot be included in the school curriculum." In this reply I heard echoes of the mid-20th century arguments about whether literature, art, law, and religion are or are not forms of knowledge. A great deal was thought to hinge on the outcome of these debates, for it was assumed that if something failed the knowledge test, it could not be allowed into the curriculum. Frankena was right, however. There is no reason whatsoever to accept the narrow conception of curriculum—or, for that matter, of education—that this line of argument presupposes.

Needless to say, care, concern, and connectedness to others all involve knowledge, be it of another's needs and desires or of the effects of one's actions on that other person. But to recognize that one who possesses a virtue must have some knowledge is not to say that the virtue itself *is* knowledge. The day Abraham Lincoln walked all those miles to return the pennies to the storekeeper, he knew that the storekeeper had given him too much change. But his honesty consisted in far more than this belief or any others. When Harriet Tubman led slaves to freedom, she had in her possession a number of facts about the Underground Railroad and also knew that there was no slavery in Canada. Still, her courage outran this and any other portion of knowledge.

Some would argue, as that young man actually tried to do, that to be honest or courageous or tolerant of differences or concerned about the planet is simply to know that one should be honest or that courage is admirable or that the planet needs all the help it can get from humankind. But there is a great gap between items of knowledge like these and the associated virtues. In human virtues, as in all human practices, knowledge, reason, feeling, emotion, and action are mixed together. As a consequence, these items of cultural wealth do not reduce to knowledge—not even when knowledge is defined broadly.

I am not saying that the portion of cultural stock that is valuable enough to pass down to the next generation includes *no* knowledge. My point is simply that although some of our wealth takes the form of knowledge, our assets include other sorts of things as well. I also want to stress that knowledge itself is a many-splendored thing. Philosophers distinguish between *knowing how* or *skill knowledge*—for example, knowing how to ride a bicycle or play the piano—and *knowing that* or *propositional knowledge*, for instance, knowing that Boise is the capital of Idaho or that Ophelia is a character in Shakespeare's *Hamlet*. And they differentiate both types of knowledge from *knowledge by acquaintance*—the direct knowledge one has of people, pets, places, pieces of music, and the like. Yet when school critics and reformers draw up lists of what every American needs to know, they seem to have in mind only the one sort—propositional knowledge. There are, then, various kinds of knowledge and various types of stock to pass down to the next generation and many things besides knowledge.

Once educational agency is decentralized and all a culture's institutions are acknowledged to be educational agents, the question arises of how the various agents are to be identified—or individuated, to use the philosopher's lingo. Is each TV network an educational agent in its own right, or is the industry as a whole one big agent? Is each art museum a separate agent, or are art museums as a class a single agent? There is no one correct answer to each of these queries, nor can they be satisfactorily answered in the abstract. The way educational agents are individuated will depend on one's interests and purposes, which means that it will vary from one context to another. If, for example, a person's main concern is whether a particular museum is transmitting negative messages about an ethnic or racial minority, it will be appropriate to consider that museum—or perhaps a particular department of that museum—an educational agent. If, in contrast, someone wants to know what portion of a culture's stock is being passed down by its museums as opposed, say, to its schools, it may be far more appropriate to designate the entire set of that culture's museums as such.

Regardless of how the educational agents of a culture are individuated, each such agent is a guardian of some portion of cultural stock. Of course, over time both the amount and the type of stock in a given agent's custody will change. On the one hand, an educational agent may acquire new stock and dispose of or misplace or lose old stock. Thus, a private collector can bequeath his or her holdings to an art museum, a symphony orchestra can commission a new cello concerto, a publisher can take a book off its lists, volumes can be stolen from a library, a national park can add a reconstruction of an American Indian village. On the other hand, with the passage of time the value of any given portion of stock can rise or fall. For example, new data may discredit a scientific theory, or the value of a Mayan vase—formerly classified as primitive art but newly described as fine art—may increase.

It may be wondered if the fact that every educational agent has some cultural stock in its keep means that every custodian of cultural stock is an educational agent. Certainly, wherever there are people or things there will be opportunities for learning—or *learning affordances*, as I will call them.[1] Wherever there are learning affordances there is, in turn, curriculum—be it intended or unintended, manifest or hidden. And wherever there is curriculum there is an educational agent. Think of an archive that does no business. It preserves the letters and journals stashed away on its shelves without their ever being read. Nevertheless, its architecture transmits myriad messages to those who work there, and so do the archivists themselves.

Given the ubiquity of learning affordances, it is safe to say that every guardian of cultural stock is an educational agent. But this is not to say that every educational agent has sole custody of the stock in its keep. Think, for example, of the Brahms Requiem or Beethoven's symphonies. Orchestras, recording companies, music publishers, radio stations, music schools, and conservatories presently have joint custody of this wealth. Think of the vast literature on women's history. Universities, schools, libraries, bookstores, and historical societies are just some of its guardians. Furthermore, if perchance an educational agent does have sole custody of some portion of stock, there is no reason to think that this arrangement will persist. Just as our culture's stock changes over time, so do its guardians. And as a guardian changes, its custodial arrangements will very likely change.

CUSTODY; OR, THE BENEFITS AND
RISKS OF JOINT VENTURES

At a 1998 string quartet concert I was so impressed by the new composition they had performed that when I spotted the composer during the intermission, I went up to speak to him. After I congratulated him both on the piece itself and on its having just been played, he told me with great pleasure that he did not own it any more; that the quartet now owned it. And to my utter surprise he then referred to the group as the "custodian" of his piece. A friend of the composer who had joined our conversation asked if this was a good thing, to which the man replied that he could now die tomorrow. "You're right, you're right," I said. Acting as interpreter, I

---

[1] I am indebted to Alexander Goldowsky for this term.

turned to the friend and said: "He means that his composition won't die. Because of this musical organization, it will live on."

I call a culture's educational agents the *guardians* of some portion of cultural stock to highlight their custodial function vis-à-vis the wealth. The "guardian" label marks the fact that the stock in an educational agent's keep is not as a rule its own private property to dispose of as it wishes. Yes, Harvard University owns the books in the stacks of Widener Library and the paintings on the walls of the Fogg Museum. But Widener's cultural stock includes far more than the volumes on its shelves. At the very least, the high ceilings, massive staircases, and musty stacks transmit messages about the exalted status of academic books and the separation of higher learning from the "real" world. Furthermore, to own a collection of books is not to be the author of any one of them, let alone to own the ideas or concepts contained therein. The opening theme of Beethoven's Fifth Symphony, the theory of relativity, Turner's Frontier Thesis—not to mention hedge laying, the three Rs, the three Cs of care, concern, and connection: I could go on indefinitely listing cultural assets that are no one's private property but are held in trust for future generations by educational agents.

To designate a given institution as the guardian of some portion of cultural wealth, then, is neither to imply that it owns the cultural stock in its keep nor to name the stock's origin. I do not simply mean that a museum may not inform the public—or may not even know—that a given vase in its vaults was stolen from a Mayan burial site or that a painting on its walls was smuggled out of its country of origin. The issues arising in these cases are enormously complex, but the one that bears most directly on this discussion is that by their very nature, museums are custodians of cultural stock that did not originate with them. And so, to be sure, are opera companies and symphony orchestras and, of course, schools. True, in taking custody of a portion of stock, museums, schools, and the rest put their own stamp on it. Still, the stock they now have was not theirs to begin with any more than the Brahms Requiem began life with the Boston Symphony Orchestra or evolutionary theory originated in the nation's public schools.

From our composer's standpoint, the very best scenario would be for more and more musical groups to share custody of his composition. That way the piece's prospects of survival would increase considerably. In cases of shared custody, if for one reason or another one guardian of a given item of stock stops preserving and transmitting it to future generations, there will be other guardians to continue the effort.

Shared custody is in fact a common occurrence, but it is not always the rule—not even for stock with a long history. In *The Schoolhome* (Martin, 1992) I argued that because of the social transformation of home and family in the last decades of the 20th century, home is no longer able to fulfill the educational responsibilities our culture long ago assigned it. Relying tacitly on the concepts of cultural wealth and multiple educational agency that I am outlining here, I proposed that school step into the breach and begin to share responsibility with home for transmitting the domestic wealth that was in home's keep. In other words, having found no evidence that some other responsible and effective educational agents shared custody of the cultural wealth in home's keep, I recommended that school and home embark on a joint venture.

Only after writing that book did I fully realize that school is not the only educational agent that should begin shouldering responsibility for stock in another guardian's keep. Indeed, it now strikes me as imperative that even as school enters into a joint venture with home, it must begin to share some of its present custodial responsibilities with other educational agents.

In some countries, the sharing of school's custodial responsibilities for vocational education with industry is already an established habit. As I watched a television documentary about vocational education in the United States, Germany, and Japan, what initially impressed me most was how well the German and Japanese programs were structured and how effective they appeared to be, especially in comparison to my own country's. I was soon struck, however, by the fact that the success of the German and Japanese systems appeared to be due to the partnerships that had been forged between school and industry. Whereas school in the United States was trying to go it alone, in both Germany and Japan vocational education was seen as a joint venture.

And so, too, science education can be treated as a joint venture involving schools, museums, and technological companies. Social studies education can be viewed as a collaborative effort in which schools, political parties, and grass-roots groups all participate. Education in the arts can become a joint project of school, symphony orchestras, opera companies, ballet troupes, fine arts museums. And so on. Of course, some such sharing already occurs. However, the parties to it are usually perceived as school's helpers rather than as educational agents in their own right.

San Francisco's Exploratorium is a fine example of the kind of shared custody I have in mind. As its biographer pointed out, the museum has never had a separate education department because it "as a whole is dedicated to teaching and learning, and that is what everyone at the museum does" (Hein, 1990, p. 125). Founder Frank Oppenheimer always insisted "that museums are educational institutions and . . . that there is no essential difference between the preservation of culture by museums and its transmission by education" (p. 146).

Yet will school still *be* school if it shoulders responsibility for a different portion of our cultural wealth? If one learns nothing else from the writings of educational historians, one discovers that education in general and schooling in particular are as subject to change, as much a part of the societal flux, as everything else. Thus, to suppose that school has some immutable task or function that it and only it must carry out, or that it can have in its custody one and only one small portion of our heritage, is to attribute to school an essential nature it does not possess. Yes, school can become guardian to different forms of cultural wealth. It can also shed or share time-honored custodial duties without losing its identity. After all, those old responsibilities were themselves once brand new.

In an earlier period in U.S. history, the community cooperated with home and family by elaborating on their teachings. Now the tables have been turned and home tends to be regarded simply as school's helper in the educational process—and a very minor one at that. I do not for a moment mean to suggest that with new custodial duties, school will need no more help. My point is that when school itself is seen as one among many educational agents, it will no longer be in a position to treat the aims and procedures of other institutions as automatically subordinate to its own. It will no longer be able to reduce home's educative role to that of proctoring children's homework—or, for that matter, reduce industry's educational function to that of providing expensive equipment.

If school loses its monopoly over educational agency when the whole nation's cultural institutions are acknowledged to be custodians of the wealth, it nevertheless stands to gain from the changed perspective. No longer will school be expected to "do it all." No longer will the sins of omission and commission of other educational agents be blamed on it. Moreover, once the fact of multiple educational agency is accepted and a new division of educational labor is worked out, school will be in the enviable position of being able to count on the collaboration and cooperation of genuine partners in the educational process.

In the course of formulating a concept of economic development as freedom, economist Amartya Sen wrote that he was providing "a perspective in which institutional assessment can systematically occur." We have to view institutions together, he said, "to be able to see what they can or cannot do in combination with other institutions. It is in this integrated perspective that the different institutions can be reasonably assessed and examined" (1999, p. 142). He might just as well have been talking about a cultural-wealth perspective on education. For only when we look at educational agencies together—only when we take an integrated perspective—can they reasonably be examined and assessed.

One vital step in ushering in an era of cooperation across the whole range of cultural custodians is the acknowledgment that school has much to gain from treating other educational agents as partners rather than as humble assistants or else dangerous rivals. Another such step is the acceptance of the principle of accountability by the whole range of educational agents. And a beginning to holding agents accountable for the damage they do in preserving and transmitting cultural liabilities is to insist that they define themselves as educational agents and to make public their actual status as such.

But we must not move too quickly here, for joint educational ventures are not all of a piece. The explicit mission of some of this nation's cultural institutions may be in fundamental conflict with the mission of others. Just think, for example, of the mission of the Ku Klux Klan or neo-Nazi organizations as opposed to those of public schooling in a diverse, democratic society. Consider the way many TV networks counteract school's efforts to teach reading by proceeding on the assumption that their audience is practically illiterate. Compare home's desire for children to become sexually responsible adults with the licentiousness purveyed by advertisers and the electronic media.

Furthermore, and very important, even when an institution seems especially well suited to undertake a joint venture, care must be exercised lest self-serving aims take precedence over educational responsibilities. On a recent plane trip I heard one man tell another that his son's school had distributed sales samples to the parents at its annual parent–teacher meeting. "You know—toothpaste, detergents, that sort of thing. It was a great sales gimmick. I only wish I had thought of it." I can all too easily imagine school entering into a joint venture with an industrial partner only to find the latter showing its commercials in school's media outlets and otherwise deliberately transmitting the values of uncaring consumerism in the guise of vocational education; a political partner of school trying to recruit new members to the party while collaborating in the teaching of social studies; a religious partner attempting to proselytize while helping school teach church history.

When Mill wrote that education and opinion should see to it that "a direct impulse to promote the general good be one of the habitual motives of action" (1863/1962, p. 269), he was talking about individuals. A cultural-wealth perspective on education suggests that the same policy needs be applied to institutions. I do not say that an automobile manufacturer should curb its desire for immediate profits in order to become an educational agent. On the contrary, the reason it must learn to subordinate its private, selfish interests and purposes to the general good is that an automobile manufacturer already *is* an educational agent.

The question remains of whether airlines and TV networks, museums and talk shows, the Internet and sports organizations can bring what Mill would term their "private pleasures" into line with the common good and remain airlines, TV networks, and the rest. Does an automobile manufacturer sacrifice its very essence when it reins in its desire for immediate profits? Does a political party change its identity if it momentarily curbs its craving for new members?

Just as school and home are subject to change, so are the other institutions of society. If school and home have no eternal, immutable nature, then neither do corporations, churches, and political parties. To be sure, one who reduces all businesses to moneymaking enterprises, political parties to vote-getting operations, and religious organizations to conversion machines will disagree. But in ignoring the fact that they do educate—and miseducate—young and old alike, reductive conceptions of a culture's institutions are at best misleading and at worst duplicitous. It goes without saying that in bringing private pleasures into line with the public good, some of these entities will undergo significant change. It should also be evident that because this change is mandated by their preexisting status as educational agents of the culture as a whole, when it occurs they will have reached a new maturity in which they are finally living up to their responsibilities.

Once again caution is required, for there is a thin line between an educational agent's acting for the common good and its simply saying it does so while in fact it pursues its own selfish ends. Museums have been attacked for acquiring stolen or otherwise ill-gotten artifacts. The issues are extraordinarily complicated, and I would not dream of taking sides in the disputes. To illustrate the difficulty of deciding whether an educational agent's actions match its claims of acting for the common good, I do, however, quote what the director of Harvard University's art museums reportedly told the press. To the suggestion that plundered artifacts should be returned to their country of origin he said: "It's out of the ground. . . . It's out of the country [of origin]. We're a public institution. Our job is to encourage research and preservation. If you don't acquire it, where would it go? Back to the netherworld of private holdings in conditions inimical to its preservation." He then continued: "What really is best for the world? Return the items and reinforce a parochial, atomized view of world culture or encourage the exposure of these items to scholarship elsewhere?" (Robinson & Yemma, 1998, p. A13).

That it can be very difficult to determine whether an institution is or is not bringing its private interests into line with the common good should not deter us from extending the moral stance Mill proposed for individuals to the culture's educational agents. The complexities do, however, mean that rather than rely on verbal references to the general welfare, one must examine each case on its own merits. Moreover, the museum director's words indicate just how much room there is for legitimate differences of opinion about what, from a cultural perspective, should be done. Should art and artifacts be in the custody of public museums rather than in "the netherworld of private holdings"? Is this even a fair contrast? In light of the fact that over a 20-year period Stephen Carrie Blumberg stole 18,900 books from libraries and museums in the United States and Canada (Reed, 1997) and that in 1973 thieves walked off with close to 12,000 coins housed in the Coin Room of Harvard's Fogg Museum (Reed, 2000), is the presumption that public guardians take good care of the artifacts in their keep justified?

Certainly, public institutions do not always take as good care of the stock in their custody as they might. Moreover, an educational agent need not belong to the netherworld of robbers, smugglers, and shady dealers to betray its cultural trust of preserving the wealth and transmitting it to future generations. In passing along cultural liabilities in lieu of assets, television networks do so daily. In refusing to take custody of the new scholarship on women and minorities, universities do likewise. In transmitting the wealth in their keep in a biased manner, so do a host of other educational agents.

I do not want to give the impression that every failure to preserve or transmit wealth or every success in passing along liabilities constitutes a betrayal of trust. Given the great social transformations of the 20th century, home's inability to preserve the culture's domestic wealth is not its fault. Farmers are not to blame for the social, economic, and technological trends that have made them unable to continue to transmit the old agricultural know-how. Moreover, what counts as a betrayal of trust depends at least in part on the way an agent's trust is defined.

Except in very special circumstances, one state's historical society has no obligation to take custody of another state's materials. If, however, the historical society's mission is to preserve its state's history, one would expect it to have in its custody materials about women inhabitants as well as men—and if it does not, one would want it to move to acquire such with all deliberate speed. But suppose—as feminist scholars in the 1970s demonstrated to be the case—that history is defined so as to include the traditional activities of men and exclude those of women. Is the historical society then justified in neglecting the lives and experiences of women? I would say that when an agent's definition of its trust turns out on examination to be arbitrarily exclusionary or systematically discriminatory, the definition itself must be rejected. Much the same thing can be said of museums, symphony orchestras, theater companies, recording studios, and of course schools.

DIVIDED LABOR; OR, THE CASE
OF OPERA NEW ENGLAND

When I was in junior high school, my classmates and I and thousands of other New York City schoolchildren attended a Metropolitan Opera House matinee performance of *Hansel and Gretel*. My main recollection of the joint venture of school and the Met to transmit a bit of the culture's wealth to the younger generation is that the stage crew forgot to place on stage the birdcage in which the witch locks Hansel and the oven into which Hansel and Gretel ultimately push the witch. I can still remember how embarrassed for them I was when they had to wheel these by no means trivial props on in the middle of a scene. The lasting message I, for one, received that day was that even such an exalted institution as the Met can make mistakes. Yet while this is perhaps as valuable an item of cultural wealth as one could ever acquire, it certainly was not what the Met intended to transmit.

One moral I draw from the Met's memorable lapse is that we need to take into account the hidden curriculum of each of a culture's educational agents as well as each one's overt curriculum—or "curriculum proper" as I prefer to call it (Martin, 1994, ch. 8). A second moral is that we must also take seriously the division of cultural labor. After all, distributing the cultural stock in its keep to children was a sideline for the Met. Notwithstanding those school matinees, its mission was to pass down operatic wealth mainly to adults.

Using the example of the "very trifling manufacture" of pin-making, Adam Smith explained how the division of labor "occasions, in every art, a proportionable increase of the productive powers of labour" (1776/1976, p. 9). A workman, said Smith, "could scarce, perhaps, with his utmost industry" (p. 8) make 1 pin a day, certainly not 20. Yet when pin-making is divided into 18 distinct operations so that "one man draws out the wire, another straights it, a third cuts it, a fourth points it, a fifth grinds it at the top for receiving the head" (p. 8) and so on, 10 men might make as many as 48,000 pins a day.

There is no arithmetic way to calculate how many cultural assets 10 small opera companies can with utmost industry transmit in a year, no calculus for counting the wealth preserved by the Met or for comparing the efficiency of the Met's guardianship with La Scala's. Nonetheless, if one considers the vast number of institutions that have joint custody of opera-related wealth, one can discern a division of cultural labor. The question of whether it is as efficacious as Smith believed the division of economic labor to be remains open. But the fact that a division of cultural labor exists for most, if not absolutely all, categories of wealth is beyond doubt.

Consider the case of opera. Despite the shameful blunder, the Met was and still remains one of the most highly regarded guardians of this parcel of cultural stock. There are, of course, many other opera companies in the Met's class, and across the world there are also untold numbers of unsung custodians of operatic wealth. These latter include not only regional and local opera companies, but recording companies, publishing houses, music stores, neighborhood music schools, nationally ranked conservatories, orchestras, choruses, radio stations, television channels, film companies, and so forth.

Although some of these guardians of opera may think of themselves as having custody of the entire body of opera-related stock, each one actually has in its keep only a portion of all the opera-related assets there are. Thus, some of opera's trustees participate in the division of cultural labor by staging only comic operas, only Wagner's operas, or only contemporary operas. There are also guardians who devote themselves to preserving and transmitting components of opera rather than entire works. Whereas the Met generally presents full-scale opera performances, some groups stage concert versions of operas and others take custody only of opera stories or scores or arias. In addition, our culture's operatic stock embraces not just operas but the myriad facts and theories about opera. Accordingly, some of opera's guardians devote themselves simply to the preservation and transmission of opera histories or biographies or interpretations or analyses.

These examples of divided labor all relate to the kind of operatic stock being preserved, but the selfsame processes can be seen at work in the stock's distribution. Just as the Met and many other guardians of this portion of the culture's stock seek to transmit their holdings to adults, other custodians of opera make it their business to pass these assets down to children. Opera New England, also known as ONE, belongs to this latter category. Founded as an arm of Sarah Caldwell's Opera Company of Boston, then reorganized as an independent entity, and since merged with the Boston Lyric Opera Company, ONE has established itself in the New England area as a guardian of operas having special appeal for children.

Wanting to know more about ONE, in the spring of 1998 I went to see its president, Linda Cabot Black. After a long conversation in which we traded information about her organization and my cultural-wealth perspective on education, she generously gave me access to some of the documents in ONE's archives. My reading of these made me far more aware than I had so far been of the vital role that the division of cultural labor plays in the preservation and transmission of cultural stock. My brief, unsystematic study of ONE also confirmed my hypothesis that a cultural object—in this case an opera—pulls many seemingly disparate items of cultural stock into its orbit.

To be specific, in 1998 ONE's repertory consisted of: Humperdinck's *Hansel and Gretel*, Mozart's *The Magic Flute*, Rossini's *The Barber of Seville*, and Lukas Foss's *The Jumping Frog of Calaveros Country*. It is, however, a mistake to think of ONE simply as the guardian of a handful of operas, for at that time it also preserved and transmitted information *about* opera. Thus the schoolchildren to whom ONE was passing down *Hansel and Gretal* went to the opera in a state of high preparation. Under ONE's guidance, they were provided with a definition of opera, an account of the origin and development of opera and of opera's construction, a list of the main types of opera, a composer chronology, a biography of Humperdinck, a description of the writing of *Hansel and Gretel*, and an analysis of the opera's relationship to fairy tales.

ONE acted as a guardian of opera-related attitudes and values as well as information. In particular, it deliberately sought to transmit to children the feeling or sense of opera as pleasurable. Contrary to what some might think, not all custodians of operatic wealth lay claim to this value. Indeed, one introductory volume on opera on my bookshelves warns the reader at the outset: "Don't expect opera simply—or even always—to entertain you" (Pettitt, 1998, p. 9). My examination of archival materials revealed that ONE considered itself the custodian of quite another value, too—namely, ethnic diversity. Of course, research is needed to determine whether it succeeded in transmitting this or the other stock in its portfolio to the next generation. My purpose here is simply to mark the diversity of the stock in ONE's keep.

Numbering operas, opera-related information and knowledge, a wide range of attitudes and values, and perhaps other kinds of cultural wealth as well, the stock in ONE's keep can be thought of as comprising a diversified portfolio, albeit one limited in scope. So, I submit, does the stock in the keep of most guardians. And although there is bound to be some overlap in the stock of the myriad guardians of opera—after all, ONE is not the only institution devoted to the preservation and transmission of *Hansel and Gretel* or to the value that the experience of opera is pleasurable—we can also expect to find that the principle of divided labor applies to all the kinds of opera-related stock there are.

Now, unlike many guardians of the culture's wealth, ONE explicitly defined its mission as educational. But if the tale of my matinee at the Met teaches a single lesson, it is that the learning generated by an educational agent's hidden curriculum can be every bit as significant and lasting as that generated by its curriculum proper—possibly far more so. Thus, the fact that ONE had a curriculum proper of its own does not mean that its hidden curriculum can be ignored with impunity. Extensive research of a kind that goes well beyond the reading of archival materials is required to discover exactly what ONE's or the Met's or any other educational agent's hidden curriculum is. I do not pretend to know the outcome of such inquiries in advance, but I have no doubt whatsoever that this kind of investigation is important to undertake.

In the last century, school critics and reformers proceeded on the assumption that a hidden curriculum is necessarily harmful, even destructive. But this need not be so. Like a curriculum proper, a hidden curriculum can generate undesirable learning, worthwhile learning, or some of each. It can also conflict with or be consonant with a given educational agent's curriculum proper. In view of all the educational agents there are, the prospects of determining each one's hidden curriculum are a bit daunting, to say the least. They are all the more so when one acknowledges that inquiries into the hidden curricula of our culture's educational agents must be ongoing—for the simple reason that as an educational agent changes over time, so does its hidden curriculum. Nevertheless, if we are ever to hold the culture's educational agents accountable, we will need to know which, if any, of an institution's actions or practices cohere with and even bolster up what it is seeking to accomplish and which unwittingly generate beliefs or values that stand in opposition to its explicit educational agenda—assuming it has one.

ONE's president told me several times in the course of our conversation that in producing operas, she and her organization become storytellers. Since some opera stories are far more appropriate for schoolchildren than others, the organization's decision to distribute operatic wealth to some of the youngest members of the next generation—specifically to children in grades 2–6—helps determine which operas it holds in trust. That ONE's mission is to pass down the wealth to schoolchildren also determines the length of the performances it puts on. The Met and La Scala may make some cuts in the operas they perform and even rearrange some scenes, but for the most part they stage entire operas. ONE, on the other hand, presents hour-long versions of the operas in its repertoire. And herein lies another philosophical puzzle.

From a practical standpoint in which school schedules and finances loom large, it makes good sense for ONE to abridge its operas. From a cultural-wealth perspective, however, the question arises of whether ONE's performances of *Hansel and Gretel* really are performances of *Hansel and Gretel*. Are they perhaps so different from standard performances that we should withhold the *Hansel and Gretel* label? To put the question another way, can ONE really be considered a cultural guardian of *Hansel and Gretel* or should it instead be considered the creator and custodian of a brand-new item of cultural wealth, namely a one-hour version of *Hansel and Gretel*?

The puzzle, which is really a version of our old friend the problem of identity, is not confined to ONE's case. It might well be asked whether the

July 1998 performance by the New England Marionettes of *Madame But-terfly*, which my husband and I attended, was really a performance of *Madame Butterfly* or whether the company had created a new item of cultural wealth, namely, a marionette version of this work. For that matter, leaving the realm of opera, we can ask whether a comic-book version of *Moby Dick* is still *Moby Dick*, whether a five-minute, speeded-up *Hamlet* is really *Hamlet*, and whether the Public Broadcasting System's version of *Middlemarch* was *Middlemarch*.

The fact that the type of stock in ONE's custody is a performing art complicates the problem of the identity of the wealth in its keep. At first glance it would seem that *Hansel and Gretel* and the other operas ONE was presenting on a rotating basis represented the major part of the wealth it was preserving and transmitting. However, what was being performed on any given occasion was not an opera pure and simple, but a production thereof. ONE did not present all the productions of *Hansel and Gretel* there have ever been, let alone all there could be. It could not possibly stage them all, nor could any opera company do or want to do so. As it happens, ONE presented Sarah Caldwell's production of *Hansel and Gretel*. But then we must ask if ONE had taken custody of *Hansel and Gretel* or merely of Sarah Caldwell's production of *Hansel and Gretel*.

This question can no more be decided in the abstract than can the one about the individuation of educational agents. Nor is it likely that there is one right answer to it. There may well be contexts and purposes in which it is important—perhaps even necessary—to identify the wealth as one or another production of *Hansel and Gretel*—or *The Magic Flute*, as the case may be. In other contexts it may make much better sense to identify the cultural wealth as the operas per se. The question also brings to the surface the highly contested philosophical problem of the metaphysical status of works in the performing arts and of the relationship between such works, their performances, and their productions. Fortunately, these issues need not be decided here. One great value of a cultural-wealth approach to education is that it is flexible enough to accommodate different judgments about profound philosophical issues.

LIVING LEGACIES AND DEAD RELICS;
OR, DEGREES OF PRESERVATION AND
MECHANISMS OF TRANSMISSION

One of the first things I did upon arriving in London in June 1984 was to visit the National Portrait Gallery. I had just completed *Reclaiming a Conversation* (Martin, 1985), and a scholar friend had told me that in this gem of a museum hung a wonderful painting of one of the parties to the historical conversation about women's education that I had reconstructed. But when I entered the room to which Mary Wollstonecraft's date of birth consigned her, she was nowhere to be seen.

Upon inquiring as to Wollstonecraft's whereabouts, a museum guard ushered me into the next room. "That is not the author of *A Vindication of the Rights of Women*," I remonstrated. "That is her daughter, Mary Wollstonecraft Shelley. She wrote *Frankenstein*." "Oh," replied the man in tones designed to soothe. "You must be looking for Mrs. Godwin. She used to be in the room you just passed through, but they have put her in storage. Would you like to see her? I'm sure it can be arranged." And the next thing I knew, I was sitting atop a high ladder in an immense warehouse of portraits, gazing into my heroine's eyes.

To say that an educational agent is guardian of some portion of cultural stock is not to specify the form in which those assets or liabilities are preserved. True, the Harvard University museum director contrasted the netherworld of private holdings with the presumed haven—or heaven—of public institutions. But even if the contrast is valid, we know better than to assume that all the stock in a public museum's keep is accorded the same respect and treated in the same way. There is a world of difference between a portrait hanging in England's National Portrait Gallery and stashed away in that museum's huge storage facility, a world of difference between a ballet in a dance company's repertory and on a videotape in its library.

From a purely logical point of view, it is perfectly legitimate to think of cultural preservation in either–or terms: either Balanchine's ballets; the old farmer's know-how; the three Cs of care, concern, and connection; the operas in ONE's keep preserved as living legacies or preserved as dead relics. But empirically speaking, the form that cultural preservation takes is perhaps better characterized as a matter of degree.

Consider this scenario: The culture is the United States, the guardian is school, the cultural stock is *Moby Dick* and *Our Eyes Are Watching God*, and the time is the 1940s to the 1970s. Asked to compare these two works of literature in regard to their form of preservation, observers readily agree that the preservation of Herman Melville's novel more closely approximates a living legacy than that of Zora Neale Hurston's novel. Asked next to compare *Moby Dick* with the Old and New Testaments, these same observers will say that the form of preservation of the latter approximates a living legacy even more closely. Granted, these judgments will be intuitive, but there is nothing wrong with that. So are the rankings of height one makes when, walking down the street, one notices that this person is taller or shorter than that one. So are our rankings of temperature when we say that one day is much hotter or colder than another. What matters is that the intuitions of different observers—and of the same observer on different occasions—agree with one another. To be sure, intuitive discriminations of height or temperature will be less precise than ones that employ yardsticks or thermometers. But it is not necessary to give a "more-or-less" concept a quantitative rendering if all that is desired is to rank order one's objects of interest reliably.

I leave it to future investigators to construct a cultural-preservation equivalent of the scratch test for hardness, if one be thought necessary; or an even more precise system than the scratch test to measure cultural preservation, if one be deemed practicable. In the meantime, I propose that we think of both cultural assets and liabilities as falling along an educational agent's *preservation continuum* whose two poles are dead relic and living legacy.

The location of any item of cultural stock on a given continuum is, of course, an empirical question. One cannot simply infer this from the fact that the stock is, say, an opera or a portrait or a ballet or a set of agricultural techniques or an ancient people's burial practices. Nor, I should add, can one infer a stock's location on a preservation continuum from the identity of the stock's guardian. I suppose it is possible for all the stock in one educational agent's keep to be at precisely the same point on its continuum. I would not be surprised to discover, however, that differentiation is the rule: that it is far more likely for one guardian's parcel of cultural stock to be distributed along its continuum than to cluster in one spot. Once again, however, this issue is not to be decided in advance of inquiry.

Whether or not the form of preservation of any given item of stock is identical in cases of shared custody is also an empirical question. I see no reason to assume that a given portion of stock will be preserved in the very same form by different guardians. Who knows, perhaps all the custodians of the Brahms Requiem preserve it as a living legacy. But I doubt this can be said of Fyodor Chaliapin's singing or Amy Beach's compositions. And even where uniformity prevails, there is no guarantee that it will persist over time. Just as the items of stock in an educational agent's custody can change, so can the form in which they are preserved.

Yet no matter how precise our knowledge of where an item of stock falls on some guardian's preservation continuum, it is quite another matter to know the *manner* in which that stock is held by its recipients. When, for example, the type of stock at issue is information—for instance, arithmetic facts or the dates of the U.S. Civil War—it is an open question whether what the legatees have acquired constitutes rote knowledge or whether it takes the form of understanding. When the stock is a pattern of action such as driving a car or playing the piano, the question remains whether the beneficiaries hold it as a more or less automatic habit or as a form of intelligent behavior.

The ambiguity inherent in any listing of the cultural stock in a guardian's keep is well illustrated by *The Dictionary of Cultural Literacy: What Every American Needs to Know* (Hirsch et al., 1988). In effect, this tome represents an inventory of the cultural wealth in the keep of the United States in 1988—or rather, an inventory of what the editors claim was then in the nation's keep. You have only to open its pages, however, to know that the entries do not in themselves answer the question: In what manner should these items of stock be held by those who inherit them? Of course, the editors may have an answer to this question. The point, however, is that the list by itself does not answer it.

Look up "Jeffersonian Democracy." Are Americans supposed to possess this concept in a rote, mechanical manner, or should we have a deep understanding of it? Now turn to "ragtime." Is ragtime music—not the concept ragtime, but the music itself—to be recognized when heard? hummed at will? appreciated and enjoyed? Or is only the concept "ragtime" at issue here? And if so, is it to be recognized and readily defined? Is it to end up as rote knowledge or to be grasped with understanding? The entry "A Midsummer Night's Dream" raises similar questions. Is the play to be read? appreciated? understood? Is it to be seen? acted in? Or is the title simply to be associated in a rote manner with Shakespeare?

The dictionary teaches another lesson, too. In an interview about public broadcasting in America, a noted British actress quoted the then–U.S. first lady as saying that a nation is defined by its culture. "I thought that was a wonderful phrase," said our actress, and she added: "I do think that WGBH is the guardian, if you like, of the culture of the country" (*Expanding the Vision*, 2000). Like her, I have been going on the assumption that the guardians of a culture's wealth and, by extension, a culture's educational agencies are groups or institutions within a given society. But the dictionary editors proceeded on the different assumption that whole societies preserve and transmit cultural wealth. And so, of course, they do—which makes them cultural guardians and educational agents in their own right.

To acknowledge this is not to deny that, for instance, WGBH is a cultural guardian. Earlier I said that whether one considers all a nation's museums or just one particular museum or simply one wing thereof to be an educational agent will depend on the context of inquiry. That point needs to be extended so as to include whole societies. In other words, the issue of whether one considers an institution within the United States or the United States itself to be a cultural guardian is also a contextual matter.

Exactly what stock does a whole nation or society hold in custody? It is tempting to think of the stock on the preservation continuum of a society as the sum total of all the stock in the custody of all the educational agents within the society. Yet a strict arithmetical answer to our question will not do, because many cultural guardians preserve and transmit items of stock that are simply too idiosyncratic—too localized, too fleeting, too unrepresentative—to be considered to fall along the preservation continuum of the society as a whole. At best this sum total can be regarded as the "pool" of cultural stock from which the assets and liabilities in a society's custody are drawn. In other words, whenever reference is made to "the" culture or "the" heritage or, for that matter, "the" cultural stock on the preservation continuum of a given society, it is really to one or another selection from this source.

As a matter of fact, whether the guardian in question is a whole society or a member institution such as WGBH, the process of deciding what stock is in its keep is highly selective. Take schooling in the United States. The stock on its preservation continuum is not the sum total of that on the preservation continua of all U.S. schools, or even all public schools. It is as much an abstraction from this huge pool as is the stock belonging to the United States. Take a single school or museum. Even here selection enters into the picture. For surely, if an institution happens to transmit a particular item of stock on one given occasion and no other, this item will not normally qualify for a place on its preservation continuum.

I said earlier in connection with the problem of the individuation of educational agents that what a person considers to be an agent will depend on his or her interests and purposes. It now turns out that what one takes to fall on a given agent's preservation continuum is also a function of one's prior commitments. And there is even more to be said about the contextual nature of educational agency. As the WGBH case makes clear, an institution that in one context is treated as a cultural guardian in its own right can in another situation be considered a method or mechanism by which some more comprehensive guardian transmits its stock.

Please note that I use the language of transmission simply to denote the transfer of cultural wealth—and cultural liabilities, too—by its guardians to one or more segments of the population. I do not mean to imply by it that schools or other educational agents play a passive role in selecting the stock in their keep and determining its value. On the contrary, the portfolios of educational agents tend to be highly selective, and their choice of stock is often very arbitrary.

This point was brought home to me on a recent trip to California. After hearing quite a bit from a guide at the Hearst Castle about William Randolph Hearst's vast wealth, I asked if we were going to be told about Hearst as a publishing magnate. Saying that people are only interested in what they can see, this representative of the California State Park System proceeded to discuss the castle's furnishings, its architectural style, its grounds and wildlife, the vast wealth all this represented, and Hearst's extramarital relationship with actress Marion Davies. For reasons best known to itself, the California Park Service had evidently decided to forgo custody of an important and very relevant body of cultural wealth. A visitor to the site would never have guessed that, in the words of a recent biographer, Hearst "was as dominant and pioneering a figure in the twentieth-century communications and entertainment industries as Andrew Carnegie had been in steel, J. Pierpont Morgan in banking, John D. Rockefeller in oil, and Thomas Alva Edison in electricity" (Nasaw, 2000, p. xiv). He or she would not have dreamed that in the 1930s Hearst's newspaper audience numbered 20 million of the 120 plus million men, women, and children in the United States; that Hitler, Mussolini, and Churchill all wrote for him; that he "employed the power of the media to set the national agenda, first as a muckraking progressive trustbuster, then, in his seventies, as an opponent of the New Deal and a stalwart anti-Communist" (p. xiv).

A selective process singling out for preservation and transmission just that stock which affirmed the importance and glamour of accumulated wealth also seemed to have been operating on our bus tour. Although the tour organization appeared to take pride in being an educational agent, our driver's narrative consisted mainly of gossip about the celebrities whose homes we passed and the high price of their real estate. The region's history, economic and social significance, literary and artistic traditions did not seem to be a part of this cultural guardian's—a.k.a. educational agent's—portfolio.

Nor is the term *transmission* meant to prejudge the type of process by which the transfer of stock occurs. The Park Service at the Hearst estate offered minilectures, but the stock in its keep was also transmitted by, for instance, the strictly enforced rules regarding where to walk and how to take photographs, as well as by the gaping holes in the narratives.

I also use the term *mechanism* in its most general sense, that is, as the means by which the transfer is, or is intended to be, accomplished. The *transmission mechanisms* at an educational agent's disposal range from deliberately designed, widely accepted educational activities such as teaching and training, instructing and explaining, lecturing and demonstrating; to equally deliberate but often-condemned ones such as indoctrination and brainwashing; to less formal but very effective transmitters of cultural assets and liabilities. No doubt some will say that a culture's liabilities cannot be part of an *educational* agent's repertoire. But were they to insist that educational activities are intentional, goal-oriented, and rationalistic by definition, I would reiterate that a broad concept of cultural wealth requires a comparably broad and decentralized conception of educational agency.

I once tried to compile a list of all the sources of school's hidden curriculum. On my list were school's rules, its social structure, its physical layout, the role models it provides, teacher–pupil relationships, the games played, the sanctioned activities, textbooks and audiovisual aids, furnishings and architecture, disciplinary measures, timetables, tracking systems, curricular priorities. I finally came to realize that I had set myself a never-ending task. New practices, procedures, and environments carry with them new learning affordances. And since school is forever changing, the list of school's transmission mechanisms will have no clear end.

The lesson I learned about school can be generalized. Of course, a given agent may avail itself of only a small sampling of the totality of transmission mechanisms. Still, there is no telling in advance just how extensive an educational agent's repertoire is. Nor in advance of research can one definitively match up cultural stock and transmission mechanisms, for a given asset or liability can be passed along by different mechanisms even as different items of cultural stock are transmitted by the same mechanism.

To complicate matters further, the transmission mechanisms for a particular item of cultural stock can change over time. Certainly, if an educational agent undergoes significant alteration, its transmission mechanisms are likely to be affected. Think, for example, how libraries have changed over the years. In 1806 the very first rule of a library in Beverly, Massachusetts, was that it should contain no novels, romances, or plays (Carpenter, 1996, p. 20). Yet by the 1870s libraries in both the North and the South were ordering titles such as *Barbara's History* and *Sybil's Second Love* from booksellers' catalogues. And collections are not the only elements of libraries that have changed radically. Both the experience of choosing, borrowing, and returning books and the library social experience are very different from what they used to be. Of course, it would be rash to suggest that every change in libraries translates into new transmission mechanisms. Think, however, of the switches from card catalogues to computerized systems; from collections of the approved classics to ones dominated by popular books of the day; and from silent, musty reading rooms to noisy, open spaces that function as community centers—surely these carry with them new ways of transmitting the culture's stock.

How convenient it would be if there were a one-to-one correlation between the forms of cultural preservation and the mechanisms of cultural transmission, but no such pattern exists. Take the Brahms Requiem. This can be passed down to future generations as a living legacy by means of recordings, live performances, television specials, FM radio orgies, and so on. What holds true for Brahms—namely, that alternative transmission mechanisms are compatible with a given form of cultural preservation—holds true for cultural stock in general.

Furthermore, and very important, what in one context counts as an educational agent will in another context count as a transmission mechanism. Indeed, in yet another it will count as an item of cultural stock. When, in his study of the decline of civic engagement in the United States, social scientist Robert Putnam calls the Boy Scouts, the PTA, the NAACP, and myriad other voluntary associations "social capital," he is including in the culture's wealth what I have been calling cultural guardians (Putnam, 2000). And well he might, for in their own right a culture's educational agents do themselves constitute an important type of cultural stock. Whether all of them can be considered wealth and therefore deserve to be called "capital" or whether some of them are definite liabilities is another matter.

On the other hand, when a whole society is considered a cultural guardian, its myriad educational agents—for instance, schools, museums, the military, the media—can equally well become the mechanisms by which the society's cultural assets and also its liabilities are passed down to the next generation. *The Dictionary of Cultural Literacy* does not mention the fact that the United States and every other nation has custody of both assets and liabilities. This needs to be said, however, for despite the positive connotations attaching to the phrase *living legacy* and the negative ones associated with *dead relic*, it is a mistake to assume that one end of the preservation continuum is preferred to the other for all items of a culture's stock. Quite the contrary. Just as humankind has tried to eradicate smallpox, so it should seek to transform rape, torture, and other cultural evils from living legacy to dead relic. And it is not only great evils and grievous sins that may warrant preservation merely as dead relic. As the members of a generation age, so do human ideas and practices. Think of gas lighting, the horse and carriage, home weaving, candlemaking. Think of the various practices suited to an agrarian economy. Because vast quantities of cultural stock become outmoded, it is only to be expected that wealth once quite properly preserved as living legacy will one day warrant removal to another place on the continuum.

CHAPTER 3

The Educational Problem
of Generations

THE PROBLEM OF GENERATIONS; OR, FROM
SOCIOLOGY TO EDUCATION

As an undergraduate I pored over Karl Mannheim's work on the role of the intelligentsia in politics. In graduate school I pondered his theory of situationally determined knowledge. Then, while writing this book, I happened upon Mannheim's "The Problem of Generations," written in the 1920s. In our earlier encounters I was not even aware that he had discussed the subject, and to be honest, if I had known, I probably would not have cared. In 1996, however, cultural transmission was very much on my mind. Remembering how opaque I had always found Mannheim's writing, I hesitated before taking the plunge. And then, for the third time in my life, Mannheim's way of constructing problems opened up new intellectual vistas.

Interpreting "the" problem of generations was akin to taking a Rorschach test. "I have gone over this maybe five times," I told a sociologist I know, "and I still have no idea what 'the' problem is—or, rather, what Mannheim took 'the' problem to be." After digging out his copy of the text and reading selected passages aloud, my friend concluded that "the" problem is how to define generations. As my readings of the essay proliferated, I became convinced that "the" problem could be any number of things.

No matter. One does not have to decide once and for all what "the" problem of generations is in order to appreciate Mannheim's achievement. After outlining 19th-century approaches to generations, Mannheim concluded that the key to understanding the problem is sociology and that sociology's task is "to work out the simplest, but at the same time the most fundamental facts relating to the phenomenon of generations" (1952, p. 287). Turning an issue that had long occupied the minds of philosophers and historians into the "sociological problem of generations"—this is what he did.

Mannheim's "The Problem of Generations" begins with a description of an experiment in imagination performed by David Hume. Suppose, Hume said, that human beings are like butterflies or caterpillars: At one stroke, the old generation disappears and another generation is born. And suppose, too, that human beings are so intelligent that each generation can choose the best form of government for itself without reference to earlier achievements. Under these conditions, there would be no need to worry about cultural continuity. It is only because generation follows generation in a continuous stream that cultural continuity is a necessity.

Presenting a hypothetical experiment of his own, Mannheim asked readers to imagine what social life would be like if one generation lived forever and no new generation took its place. In this "utopia" there would, of course, be no such thing as cultural transmission. The need to preserve the culture's assets would presumably exist, and so might the need or desire to distribute the wealth widely. But there would be no problem of having to transmit the heritage to future generations because there would be no future generations. In contrast, Mannheim said, actual human society has these characteristics:

1. New participants in the cultural process are emerging.
2. Former participants in that process are continually disappearing.
3. Members of any one generation can participate only in a temporally limited section of the historical process.
4. It is therefore necessary continually to transmit the accumulated cultural heritage.
5. The transition from generation to generation is a continuous process.

One consequence of Mannheim's formulation of the basic facts of generations is the kind of cultural loss at issue in the Balanchine controversy. A second and opposite consequence is cultural renewal. Mannheim pointed out that only if the people in his utopia had "perfectly universal minds" (1952, p. 294) would that society be in a position to compensate for the lack of the new "cultural possessions" resulting from the continuous emergence of new human beings. Were there no generations, there would be no changed relationship of individuals to cultural stock, which in turn means that there would be no cultural renewal.

There is, however, another consequence of Mannheim's basic facts, one that he overlooked. Like all analyses, his sociological formulation of the problem of generations highlighted some issues and not others. Most notably, it brought to the fore the vexing questions of whether and how the losses that inevitably occur when cultural wealth is transmitted to the new generation are to be offset. At the same time, the analysis masked what, taking a leaf out of Mannheim's own book, I will call the "educational problem of generations."

Try this experiment. Assume that one generation follows another in a continuous stream, but imagine that the whole of a culture's stock is composed of cultural wealth; in other words, there are no such things as cultural liabilities. Imagine that this wealth never becomes outdated but retains its relevance from one generation to the next. And imagine, too, that the handful of guardians of the stock all act in good faith in preserving and transmitting the wealth in their keep. In my "utopia," cultural transmission is necessary, but there is no danger that the guardians will fail to pass down the wealth and no need to separate liabilities from assets, let alone find ways of preventing the transmission of cultural liabilities. To be sure, as new generations create new cultural wealth, the problem of superabundance may become acute. Still, an embarrassment of riches is a dilemma to be enjoyed.

From a cultural-wealth perspective, one can see that, in contrast to this hypothetical situation, human society has a number of properties in addition to the characteristics Mannheim isolated. These include the following:

1. The cultural stock consists of both assets and liabilities.
2. This stock is preserved and transmitted from generation to generation by a multiplicity of guardians.
3. There is no invisible hand that makes sure the guardians of cultural stock maximize the transmission of assets and minimize the transmission of liabilities.
4. It is therefore necessary to devise ways of so doing.
5. The maximizing of assets over liabilities must be a continuous process.

Like many before and since, Mannheim spoke of the accumulated cultural heritage without saying that a society's cultural stock is composed of liabilities as well as assets. To be sure, the term *heritage* is usually reserved for that portion of stock deemed valuable. Yet the question of how to frustrate or impede the transmission of cultural liabilities remains. Perhaps there have been societies whose cultural stock included so few liabilities as to render this issue immaterial. But Mannheim's Germany was not one of them, nor, so far as I know, do any now exist. In comparison to an imaginary society that has no cultural liabilities to pass along and whose cultural guardians transmit the wealth efficiently, actual human societies face two problems—one of omission and one of commission. There is the grave danger that the older generation will fail to pass down valuable portions of its wealth, and there is the equally serious risk that it will pass down cultural liabilities instead of assets.

Two brute facts about actual human societies—the superabundance of cultural stock and the multiplicity of cultural guardians—intensify both problems. To avoid the twin sins of omission and commission, a culture needs to know the full extent of its assets and liabilities. Yet the vast amount of stock and the huge array of guardians—from art museums to drug traffickers, from pornographic publishers to Mothers Against Drunk Driving— make the taking of an inventory an extremely difficult task. That so many cultural guardians with overlapping responsibilities nonetheless work at cross-purposes further complicates the inventory process. The fact that relatively few guardians regard themselves as educational agents—and that the general population does not regard them as such—makes the project of locating assets and liabilities, identifying their respective guardians, and determining who the beneficiaries are positively daunting.

Were there an invisible hand encouraging every custodian of cultural stock to promote the greater good, there might be no need for an inventory. There would certainly be no reason to insist that the culture's custodians should acknowledge their status as educators. Indeed, there would be no problem of how to maximize the transmission of cultural assets and minimize the transmission of cultural liabilities. But actual human societies have no guardian angel.

In a single week my daily newspaper reported:

An attack on a school bus in Algeria that killed 16 children and the driver
A search for the body of a kidnapped 10-year-old Massachusetts boy
The stabbing of an elderly New Jersey woman by a home health aide who coveted her savings
A hit-and-run fatality
An epidemic of youth suicides and suicide attempts
A city that bears the scars of war

And that was long before the events of September 11, 2001. All of which is to say that the cultural stock belonging to the Western and Eastern, the Northern and Southern worlds and right now being passed down to successive generations includes murder and rape, terrorism and war, prejudice and discrimination, poverty and greed.

For a solution to the problem of maximizing the transmission of cultural wealth and minimizing the transmission of cultural liabilities, we must look to education. Some may recommend the use of force to put our cultural house in order, forgetting that in employing force the culture would be adding to its problems by transmitting one more cultural liability. But no, this problem of generations is educational—not in some narrow rationalistic sense of the term *education*, but in the broad inclusive sense that acknowledges both the educative and miseducative potential of the whole range of cultural institutions.

The problem is also urgent. If the older generation does not persuade its educational agents to prevent these liabilities from being passed down to future generations as living legacies, it may well place the next generation in cultural bankruptcy. Economists and other social analysts have been known to voice misgivings about the financial burdens my own generation has bequeathed to future ones by its military spending, its unwillingness to invest in social welfare, and its disregard of the natural environment. The cultural debt—what might just as well be called "cultural poverty"— we impose because we are unwilling to interfere with the electronic media's transmission of violence, callousness, consumerism, racism, sexism, and pornography is every bit as troubling.

THE STORYTELLERS; OR, THE SOCRATIC HYPOTHESIS

What should I find when I was clearing out my mother's closet after she died but the copy of *Heidi* that an aunt had given me as a young child. When I asked my father how my book could possibly have ended up in so unlikely a place, he told me he had hidden it there years ago. "Why on earth did you do that?" I asked in astonishment. "It was too sad," said this ardent democrat who would willingly have laid down his life to preserve his country's freedom of speech and of the press. "It made you cry," explained this parent whose prime concern had always been his child's growth and development.

"You know," said Socrates in Book II of Plato's *Republic*, "that the beginning of any process is most important, especially for anything young and tender. For it is at that time that it takes shape, and any mould one may want can be impressed upon it" (1974, 377b).[1] In Book II of *Émile*, Rousseau wrote: "The most dangerous period of human life is that from birth to the age of twelve. This is the time when errors and vices germinate

---

[1] Experts disagree over whether the Socrates of the *Republic* represents the historical Socrates or simply Plato's own prejudices. I will bracket this question here. Thus, for instance, when I say, "Socrates believed . . . ," I am using shorthand for "the Socrates of the *Republic* believes . . . ."

without one's yet having any instrument for destroying them; and by the time the instrument comes, the roots are so deep that it is too late to rip them out" (1762/1979, p. 93). Yet what error or vice could *Heidi* have caused to take root in me? Isn't the old adage true that sticks and stones can break your bones but words can never hurt you?

Socrates maintained that words can make or break you. "Shall we then carelessly allow the children to hear any kind of stories composed by anybody?" he asked. Assured that they should not, he said: "Then we must first of all . . . control the story tellers. Whatever noble story they compose we shall select, but a bad one we must reject. Then we shall persuade nurses and mothers to tell their children those we have selected and . . . the majority of the stories they now tell must be thrown out" (377b–c). When asked which stories should be discarded, he produced a long list of ones whose content was potentially harmful. And he also implicated the manner of presentation. Thus, for example, storytellers should not be allowed to imitate more than one person (398a–b) or indulge in dirges and lamentations (398c), and their songs should not be in "the lamenting modes" (399b).

As if enacting Socrates' script for the lamenting modes, my father threw *Heidi* out. There would be no groans, moans, or mumbles; no complaints, wails, or whimpers; no tears or weeping in my childhood—not if he could help it! Yet what harm could a story written in a lamenting mode do me? For that matter, what harm could be done by any of the tales Socrates wanted to throw out?

"The young cannot distinguish what is allegorical from what is not," said Socrates, "and the beliefs they acquire at that age are hard to expunge and usually remain unchanged. That may be the reason why it is most important that the first stories they hear should be well told and dispose them to virtue" (378e). One virtue whose praises he sang was self-control. "Examples of self-control in all things, in word or deed, on the part of famous men, these must be seen and heard" (390d). If, however, a young man were to hear stories containing the lamentations of famous men, "he would not be ashamed to lose his self-control and utter many groans and laments for small misfortunes" (388e). In addition, if he were told that Achilles or any other hero "ventured upon dreadful and impious deeds" (391d), he would "be ready to excuse his own evil conduct" (391e). Courage—especially in the face of death—was another virtue that Socrates extolled. Yet how can a person be without fear of death if he is told that the underworld is full of terrors? For that matter, how can people believe that it is impious to hate one's fellow citizens if tales are told of gods fighting each other? Moreover, why should each individual follow one and only one occupation—as must be done in the Just State Plato envisioned—if storytelling itself involves the successful imitation of many things? (395).

At first glance Socrates' desire to treat some stories as dead relics and to transmit others as living legacies appears to rest on a straightforward imitation theory of learning: Tell children stories of heroes running from battle and, when they grow up, they will run from battle. But the reproduction of depicted behavior is only one sort of learning at issue here. Yes, a child who is told a story may well imitate the hero's actions. But Socrates was saying that whether or not a child copies the hero's behavior, he or she is apt to acquire the belief that this behavior represents the norm or standard for all people. Furthermore, he was suggesting that a story might place its stamp on a child's feelings and emotions. In other words, it was his expressed opinion that thoughts, actions, feelings, emotions, and character itself are implanted—or perhaps one should say "imprinted"—by stories.

Two millennia and several centuries later, the Socratic hypothesis regarding storytelling is confirmed. Analyses of mid-20th century research into the relationship between pornography and aggression showed that two very different models of learning, one of them running counter to Socrates' philosophy, were then being used by investigators. Considering art and literature to be "safety valves" that release aggressive drives in harmless ways, the catharsis model made its guiding assumption: "The more you see, the less you do." Maintaining that people learn patterns of behavior from role models, the other—the imitation model—assumed precisely the opposite, namely: "The more you see, the more you do" (Bart & Jozsa, 1980, p. 205). Socrates obviously agreed with the latter assumption. If you include the expression of feelings and emotions under the rubric "the more you see, the more you do," then so, presumably, did my father when he removed *Heidi* from the scene. And so, too, do the millions who live in mortal dread of what the media in its myriad incarnations are doing to their sons and daughters.

A 1998 review of research on the impact of media violence reported that by the 1990s the catharsis model had been abandoned. Although this judgment may have been somewhat premature—in 2000 I was still coming across defenses of the media that invoked the model—the vast majority of studies now concur that media violence has debilitating effects (Bok, 1998; cf. Dickinson, 2000). Experts divide these into four categories: aggression, fear, desensitization, and appetite—otherwise known as "the aggression effect, the victim effect, the bystander effect, and the appetite effect" (Bok, 1998, p. 58).

Shades of Socrates, this! He warned that exposing the young to terrifying stories about the underworld would produce a fear of death instead of the courage they would need in order to guard and defend the state. Studies done at the end of the 20th century showed that a feeling that threats abound in the outside world is common among television viewers of all ages and that viewers who watch more than 3 hours of television a day are more likely than others to "feel at high risk of victimization from violence, take their neighborhoods to be unsafe, and regard the world as 'mean and gloomy'" (Bok, 1998, p. 62).

Socrates worried that stories depicting the wrongdoings of heroes would cause children to interpret the misbehavior as the norm or standard. A 1993 survey reported that "heavy consumers" of violent programming and movies under the age of 30 are less bothered by violence on television and less likely than others to feel that violence is harmful to society (Bok, 1998).

Socrates feared that an early exposure to stories about gods or heroes fighting with one another would cause grown citizens to act in similar fashion. Research now shows that media violence has stronger effects "when carried out by heroic, impressive, or otherwise exciting figures" (Bok, 1998, p. 85). And although most scholars do not concur with the 21% of ordinary Americans who in 1995 blamed television more than any other factor for teenage violence, they do agree that media violence "contributes to lowering barriers of aggression among at least some viewers" (Bok, 1988, p. 84).

"The aggression effect," "lowering barriers of aggression," "compassion fatigue," "desensitization": The technical vocabularies and dispassionate tone that are considered the marks of genuine scholarship tend to mask the grim realities. In the video game Night Trap, three men in black masks burst into the bedroom of a scantily clad woman. If the player does not react quickly, the men drag her off and hold her down as a fourth man plunges an electric drill into her neck. In the game Mortal Kombat, the winner can rip out a victim's spinal column. In the game Postal, players slaughter a SWAT team, a marching band, churchgoers, and bystanders. In the game Carmageddon, racing cars mow down pedestrians for points.

As of December 1997, the World Wide Web housed 60,000 sites featuring "adult material." Many members of the older generation—which is to say, my generation—assume that the "adult" label designates relatively harmless material of the kind they associate with *Playboy*. In fact, the Internet allows one and all access to the following:

Explicit photographs showing women having sexual intercourse with
    groups of men and with dogs, donkeys, horses, and snakes
Photographs of women being tortured
Photographs depicting women being raped
Photographs of women engaged in sex and made up to appear as pre-
    adolescent girls (Kelly, 1997).

In the real world, a teenage boy in Oregon goes to school one morning, opens fire in the cafeteria, kills 1 student, wounds 23 others. In Arkansas, two boys aged 11 and 13 dress in camouflage, arm themselves with rifles, and lie in wait in the woods outside their school. When a false alarm clears out the building, they shoot and kill 4 girls and a teacher and wound 11 others. In Kentucky, an armed boy goes to school, opens fire on a prayer circle in the hallway, kills 3 students, wounds 5 others. In Alaska, a 16-year-old, armed with a shotgun and a hit list, goes to school one morning, kills his principal and 1 student, wounds 2 more.

"You send your kids off to school and you never expect anything like that to happen," says a Boston area parent. "It doesn't worry me to send them to school. It worries me to send them out the door every day. It's a sick world." A woman who has moved into a safe suburban cul-de-sac declares, "I wouldn't let my children disappear for half an hour . . . with all the weird stuff going on today. You just can't be too careful" (quoted in O'Brien & Rodriguez, 1998, p. 1).

No, you cannot be too careful. In Pennsylvania, friends string a 15-year-old girl up in a tree because she threatens to reveal their plan to run away. One of them then clubs her to death. In England, a teenage girl is kidnapped, tortured, and set alight by young acquaintances. This is after two 10-year-old boys torment and then murder a toddler (Bok, 1998).

When the killings are in Arkansas, Northerners blame the South's gun culture. When they are in Oregon, authorities round up the usual suspects. School officials insist that the slaughter is a societal problem and should not be blamed on schools. The governor of Oregon wants to know "what kind of despair drives children to this kind of violence." A mayor says it is not his town's problem but society's. A parent comments that the boy obviously had problems. And when the killings are in Colorado, the U.S. House of Representatives Republican majority whip blames them on Darwin: "Our school systems teach the children that they are nothing but glorified apes who have evolutionized out of some primordial soup of mud" (quoted in Raymo, 1999, p. C2).

The different voice in this chorus of buck-passing belongs to a teenage witness of the Oregon slayings. Confirming Socrates' hypothesis that the young cannot distinguish what is allegorical from what is not, she says: "It was like a movie and you were there" (quoted in Gorov, 1998, p. A20). It belongs also to a 13-year-old Boston area boy. Reflecting on the Arkansas killings, he seconded Socrates' insight that the wrongdoings represented in stories are interpreted as the norm: "I don't think those boys understood how bad killing is. They see it all day on TV and in video games. You shoot to kill the bad guys, and it doesn't seem that bad" (quoted in Hart & Daley, 1998, p. A29). A pediatrician at Boston's Children's Hospital in turn commented that the scenario "does strongly suggest the playing out of some fantasy with military or militia symbols, and it naturally raises the question about whether it was a result of some media to which these kids may have been exposed" (quoted in Kong, 1998, p. A12).

Defenders of the media say: Do not blame the media. Blame poverty. Blame parents. Blame drugs and alcohol. Blame the availability of guns. Blame the fact that the United States is culturally predisposed to violence. In insisting that the media have a responsibility to refrain as much as possible from passing down cultural liabilities to the next generation, I do not deny that other educational agents have the selfsame responsibility. Far from it.

Homes in which domestic violence and the sexual abuse of children are rife pass down these practices to the next generation. Schools that countenance racial and ethnic epithets or bullying and the sexual harassment of girls do their fair share of transmitting cultural liabilities. So do corporations that cheat their customers and exploit their employees. These and our other educational agents should be seeking to maximize the transmission of cultural assets and stanching the flow of cultural liabilities from one generation to the next. Nevertheless, I would argue that if the United States is, indeed, culturally predisposed to violence, then the various media along with the culture's other educational agents should be doing whatever they can to neutralize this tendency. One obvious and relatively simple way would be the proliferation of the kind of believable and heartwarming programming that one occasionally encounters even now. I am speaking, in particular, of stories that portray men and women, girls and boys helping others, working together for the common good, and resolving conflicts peacefully.

Without for a moment condoning gun possession, I also want to insist that the availability of guns in the United States is one thing and the use of them to maim and kill other human beings is quite another. Thus, the media with all deliberate speed should be divesting themselves of violent stories and images of shootings.

Defenders will now say that the media necessarily reflect culture, that they do not and cannot reform it. But this is a gross distortion of the facts. Oscar Wilde is the one who said, "Life imitates art far more than art imitates life" (Tripp, 1970, 536.134). When a witness to school killings thinks she is in a movie and television viewers wonder whether the planners of the attack on New York City's World Trade Center got their idea from the mass media, that judgment is vindicated. And in any case, educational agents—and, willy-nilly, this is what the media are—are duty bound to avoid miseducating the next generation, which is another way of saying that they are duty bound to seek ways of minimizing the transmission of cultural liabilities.

THE IDEAL OF AN EDUCATIVE SOCIETY; OR,
THREE FLAWED VISIONS

The more I thought about my father's behavior toward *Heidi*, the more puzzled I became about whether it constituted censorship. On the day I presented my Heidi problem at a meeting of the small research group I belong to, I discovered that others shared my confusion. Two members of the group had absolutely no doubt that what my father had done amounted to censorship, two were equally sure that it did not, and two sat on the fence. Things got no better when the discussion turned to the definition of censorship. To every criterion of censorship suggested—for instance, that it entails governmental, not parental, action; that it involves the removal of material from the scene; that it must be done publicly; that the material in question must be judged harmful—someone raised a fatal objection.

The person in my group who was most adamant that my father had engaged in censorship likened his behavior to her own regarding her young daughter's television viewing. "Every time I refuse to let her watch a certain program, I'm acting as a censor," she told us. "No you're not," said another, "you're acting like a responsible parent." That got us started. Are parents of young children, by definition, censors? "Well, if parents are censors, then so are teachers," remarked one of our fence-sitters. "And what about librarians?" asked the other. Had I thought of it at the time, I would have added, "And what about magazine and newspaper editors, disk jockeys, book clubs, book stores, publishers, museums?"

As the discussion progressed, I saw us starting to slide down a slippery slope leading from my father's hiding *Heidi* to censorship as something that everyone does—indeed, that one cannot avoid doing. One reason I did not want to take this route is that a definition that embraces every action involving the selection of materials for others to read, view, or hear drains the term *censorship* of meaning. A host of social and political theorists have maintained that censorship is inimical to democracy. When every curriculum decision is considered to be an act of censorship; when every course syllabus, library shelf, and publisher's list is seen as a collection of such acts; when every birthday gift of a book or videotape is thought to reflect the censoring of all the other books or videotapes in the world—then censorship becomes an everyday, run-of-the-mill occurrence having no particular significance for democracy or any other form of government.

Those democratic thinkers who condemn censorship rely on a much narrower definition of the term than the one that lies at the bottom of the slippery slope. The trouble is that an adequate, uncontested formulation of their narrower sense of the term is not readily available. And in light of our group's deep disagreement about the *Heidi* problem, I now know better than to expect the definitional problem to be solved once and for all in the near future. Fortunately, a solution to the educational problem of generations does not depend on there being a generally agreed upon definition of the term *censorship*. All it requires is that we recognize clear cases of censorship—such as Plato's handling of the storytellers—when we encounter them. For the remainder of this discussion, I will therefore bracket the question "What is censorship?" and will ask instead what, if anything, can be learned from past attempts to solve our problem.

It is too much to expect the utopian vision of Plato, Rousseau, or the early-20th-century American writer and lecturer Charlotte Perkins Gilman to contain an adequate solution to a present-day problem. I would argue, however, that each of these attempts to portray a truly educative society can help us gain insight into our topic.

In fairness to my father, let me say at the outset of this venture that he was not following Plato's complete script. He never tried to banish *Heidi* from society as a whole, nor did he even want to ban it from schools and libraries, as so many people in the United States have done with books such as *The Catcher in the Rye*. Rather, in the manner of Émile's tutor, he was trying to create an educative environment in which to raise his child. And let me issue the reminder that the state or property of being educa*tive* is quite different from that of being educa*ted*. The latter is usually attributed to individual people, whereas the former is not. The relevant contrast to being educated is being *un*educated. The relevant contrast to being educative is being *mis*educative.[2] In this day and age, many would call a nation with a high literacy rate an educated society, and certainly a nation most of whose members had attained a higher degree would be so classified. However, a society—whether big or small, whether a nation state or a nuclear family—that is literate, hence educated, can be miseducative, as the cases of Nazi Germany and countless abusive homes clearly demonstrate—and so, for that matter, can a society whose every member has a Ph.D.

Both Plato and Rousseau took the educational problem of generations seriously, which is to say that both wanted to ensure that society be educative rather than miseducative. The two differed, however, in that Rousseau did not propose the elimination from society itself of all those stories that could harm Émile. Instead, he advocated the removal of Émile from society.

---

[2] I wish to thank Ann Diller for reminding me of this distinction.

"You will not be a child's master if you are not the master of all that surrounds him," mused Rousseau, as in his imagination he placed Émile in a controlled environment containing "only objects suitable for him to see"(1762/1979, p. 93). In Rousseau's opinion, books and stories were not suitable objects. He opposed any kind of verbal lessons primarily because he believed that Émile ought to acquire ideas only from experience. But his analysis of La Fontaine's fable "The Crow and the Fox" makes clear that he also took exception to stories on Platonic grounds: "Follow children learning their fables; and you will see that when they are in a position to apply them, they almost always do so in a way opposite to the author's intention, and that instead of looking within themselves for the shortcoming that one wants to cure or prevent, they tend to like the vice with which one takes advantage of others' shortcomings" (p. 115).

Determined to keep errors and vices from germinating, Rousseau tried to eliminate from Émile's childhood environment the stories, poems, and other materials that might pass along the culture's liabilities. And then he hoped for the best. His assumption was that a society need not be purged of its harmful elements because a child who has never been exposed to cultural liabilities is effectively immunized against acquiring them as an adult.

Plato was not so optimistic. Yes, Socrates said that the beginning of the process is most important. Still, he did not remove the causes of cowardice, greed, self-indulgence, and all the culture's other liabilities from children's lives and then leave the rest to chance. The "reentry problem" that confronts Émile is not an issue in the Just State, for Socrates extended his purification program to society as a whole.

Reentry is not a problem in the educative society envisioned by Charlotte Perkins Gilman either. Her 1915 utopian novel *Herland* is one of the many items of wealth pertaining to women that for years and years were missing from both official and unofficial lists of the cultural assets of the United States. In 1979 this work was retrieved and its great value made known.[3] Although *Herland* has since been highly rated for its depiction of a society composed entirely of girls and women, Gilman's imagined country has another interesting feature: It is an educative society whose shared ideal is "to make the best kind of people" (1915/1979, p. 59). The Herland dream is not the accumulation of economic wealth but the growth and development of children. This translates into a desire to perfect the environment for children; in other words, to make it as conducive to their growth and development as possible and to strive to keep it that way.

[3]Thanks to historian Ann Lane.

In striking contrast to the educative society outlined by Plato, the Herland dream does not require that harmful materials be banned. In Herland, where every adult has every child's well-being at heart, there is no need to control the storytellers or to throw out their bad stories: Every adult will of her own accord transmit only those tales that have beneficial effects. Furthermore, and again in contrast to Plato's utopia, because Herland encourages its citizens to harness their considerable reason and abundant theoretical knowledge to solve the practical problems of society, they will gladly undertake the research needed to determine which tales are likely to promote healthy development and which are likely to stunt it, and they will be quick to heed the results.

If one thinks about it, the women of Herland are in some ways more like Émile's tutor than like the philosopher kings and queens of the *Republic* whose job it is to purge society of its harmful elements. To be sure, Gilman's experiment in imagination does not require the removal of children from society: The society she envisions is separate from the rest of the world and all but impermeable to outside influences. Still, as Rousseau made a single man responsible for creating an educative environment for a single boy, Gilman made the whole population of Herland responsible for creating and maintaining an educative environment for all children.

Because Gilman equated children's educational environment with Herland itself, the girls of Herland differ from Émile in one important respect: They will not have his "reentry" problem. Émile is raised in what amounts to a laboratory situation—a relatively closed system on which the real world only occasionally impinges. Having been given little if any knowledge of how to recognize error and vice, let alone how to avoid these when encountered, Émile may not know how to cope with a wide array of educational agents bent on transmitting the culture's liabilities as well as its assets. Granted, Gilman's girls will not know either. But so long as Herland is a nation of surrogate mothers—not in the contemporary sense of putting their wombs in the services of another, but in the old-fashioned sense of loving and serving children to whom they have not given birth— their inability will not matter. If things were to change—if, for example, the Herland airwaves began to crackle with racist epithets and misogynist lyrics and satellites began beaming down images of violence and destruction—the girls in Herland would of course find themselves in Émile's position. But then, if things were to change, the inhabitants of Plato's utopia would be in trouble, too.

The truth is that any solution to the educational problem of generations that constructs a wall of separation between children and harmful materials is likely to fail if the wall should crumble and those materials reenter the scene. Since in this electronic age any such wall is bound to crumble, the reentry problem is one reason I do not cite the experiments in imagination of Plato, Rousseau, and Gilman as models to be emulated. Another is that each one has a fatal flaw.

To begin with Plato, his policy regarding storytelling is clearly at odds with the ideals and principles of an open, democratic society. Attributing infallibility to the rulers of his Just State, he took it for granted that their decisions about which stories to eliminate and which to promote could not be mistaken. However, as John Stuart Mill argued so eloquently in *On Liberty*, no matter how rational and how well educated a human being is, every single one of us is fallible. Given this brute fact of human existence, no one can know for certain that the stories deemed harmful really are; no one can be sure that beliefs we think are true—even the ones we feel absolutely certain about—are not partly or wholly false.

Mill's point about human fallibility applies to the Socratic hypothesis itself. But if we cannot be certain that it is true, should we not ignore it? Not at all. Mill pointed to the difference between "presuming an opinion to be true because, with every opportunity for contesting it, it has not been refuted, and assuming its truth for the purpose of not permitting its refutation" (1863/1962, p. 145). Thus he would say, and I agree, that so long as Socrates' hypothesis is well supported and we do not cut off discussion and criticism of it, we are free to act on it. And Mill would add that in the case of children we have special reason—perhaps even an obligation—to act. Affirming the importance of protecting growing children, Mill wrote, and again I concur: "Those who are still in a state to require being taken care of by others must be protected against their own actions as well as against external injury" (p. 135). Although Mill was not thinking in cultural-wealth terms, stories, poems, and advertisements that transmit a culture's liabilities do children external injury.

Rousseau is not usually accused of censorship, let alone of advocating policies inimical to democracy. Yet his program of controlling every detail of a child's daily existence—which is what the tutor must do to protect Émile from the myriad sources of error and vice—is totalitarian in its own right, and Rousseau's unbridled enthusiasm for deceiving and manipulating the young is self-defeating as well as morally repugnant.

As for Gilman, the fatal flaw in her solution to the educational problem of generations is her assumption that an educative society requires a homogeneous population. This not only contradicts today's realities but also denies the value of the very diversity that informs a cultural-wealth approach to education. For Gilman's is not merely a one-gender community. In excluding outsiders—which means women as well as men—Herland turns its back on the different peoples of the world as well as on the enormous range of human practices that constitute the wealth of cultures. Like Plato's *Republic, Herland* puts forward a veritable model of a closed society.

It may be wondered why I bother with these three utopian visions if they leave so much to be desired. Quite simply, each one in its own way speaks directly to the present condition of the United States and quite probably to other contemporary cultures as well. Plato's insight that a culture's stock contains both assets and liabilities and that educational agency is dispersed throughout a culture could scarcely be more relevant to our own situation. But equally germane are Rousseau's perception that a member of the older generation can act as an intermediary between a child and society, thereby protecting the child from society's miseducative tendencies, and Gilman's insight that all adults should serve this function for all children. To be sure, Gilman's surrogate mothers are women, but there is no reason why men as well as women cannot perform this function. Said Fred Rogers, host of *Mr. Rogers' Neighborhood*, a public television show for young children, "If in some little way, our neighborhood has been able to support the healthy development of what it means to be loved and accepted for who we all are, then we've done our job" (quoted in Rosenwald, 2000, p. A3).

Socrates' misgivings about storytelling presuppose a particular conceptualization of storytelling, one that assumes a simple two-way relation between story and child: Child hears story; story injures child. In placing Émile's tutor on center stage, Rousseau turned this *two-way* relation into a *three-way* relation: Child hears story *as it is mediated by an adult who has the child's growth and development at heart.* Acting as mediators between stories and children is what parents and teachers have always done. We do it when we explain or clarify or elaborate on some aspect of a story. We do it when we allay a child's fears of the villain of the piece or draw out a story's moral or simply say to the child, "It's just pretend."

There is a certain irony here. Although Socrates desperately wanted his utopia to be educative rather than miseducative, he detached stories from their pedagogical contexts. Attributing harmful powers to stories in and of themselves, he then called for their removal from society. Of course, today's technological "advances" tend to confirm Socrates' view of the matter. A child sitting in front of a television screen, looking at pornography on the Internet, or playing a computer game is all too likely to be in a direct, unmediated relation with whatever scary or violent or lascivious or racist or misogynist story the electronic medium happens to be telling. Yet this two-way relation is not engraved in stone. The story–child relation can be turned into a mediated *three-way* relation that vitiates the story's power over the child. I should say, all this can happen *provided* we join Gilman's insight to Rousseau's—*provided* we distribute the desire to maximize the transmission of cultural assets and minimize the transmission of cultural liabilities across the whole population and the whole range of the culture's educational agents.

SCHOOL AND HOME; OR, AN OBSOLETE DIVISION OF LABOR

When in the early 1970s a girl in my son's third-grade class died at home in a freak accident, the school did nothing to help the children deal with the news. The principal and her staff neither spoke to the students about the incident nor gave them opportunities to express their sorrow and fears. These school people never brought parents together to talk about the effects of the tragedy on our offspring. They did not even invite child psychologists in to advise us.

I have never doubted that the school's policy of silence was meant to be for the children's own good. In the principal's eyes, silence was the way to protect them from the injuries that stories about the bizarre death might cause. I once asked her if the children in the school were being given the opportunity to talk about the war in Vietnam that was then consuming the nation. "They are much too young to be told about the terrible things that go on in the outside world," was her reply. This is precisely what Rousseau would have said about Émile. The trouble is that my son and his friends were not removed from society as Rousseau wanted Émile to be. When they walked out the school door each afternoon, they returned to homes where they heard the war being discussed at the dinner table and could follow its progress on television. Before arriving home and hearing the tale of their classmate's death at that same dinner table, they encountered gorier versions of the story on the playground.

Yes, children need to be protected from external injury, but silence too often buys the wrong kind of protection. Living apart from society, Émile will not suffer from being kept ignorant of the world's ills until the time comes for his reentry. But most schoolchildren experience reentry on a daily basis. And because reentry so often means standing in a direct, unmediated relationship with the stories being transmitted by the media, peer groups, church, the family, and more, the protection afforded by school's silence is illusory.

In response to the media's obsession with President Clinton's sexual conduct, the director of a U.S. school sent home a bulletin to parents:

> The times require parental vigilance. In a society that is increasingly unwilling to regulate itself, parents who care must fight a lonely battle for high

standards and propriety. Explanations and discussion are important, but not enough. What children really deserve is adult protection from immersion in tantalizing yet confusing events, and ultimately, the cocoon of childhood needs to be restored. We cannot permit innocence to become passé. (Shaw, 1998, p. 1)

He was right that children deserve adult protection. However, those who at the dawn of the 21st century still pinned their hopes on parents had evidently forgotten the great social transformations that occurred in their lifetimes.

Would that parents could be eternally vigilant! Would that they could single-handedly protect their children from the culture's liabilities! Would that the desire to shield their offspring were not itself endangered by the very educational agents whose behavior threatens our young! In fact, with both men and women leaving home each day to spend long hours in the workplace, the nest is often empty when a child arrives home from school. If a parent does greet the child, he or she may have too much to do or be too exhausted to exercise the requisite vigilance. And as the research on media violence suggests, these adults may themselves have internalized the very liabilities that they do not want their children to inherit.

The school director's abiding assumption that protection is home's job, not school's, is a reflection of our culture's continued commitment to an obsolete division of educational labor. Just about all of us—parents, politicians, school and university teachers and administrators, and just plain citizens—implicitly divide social reality into the world of the private house, to use Virginia Woolf's apt phrase (Woolf, 1938), and the world of work, politics, and the professions. We then take it for granted that the function of education in general, and of schooling in particular, is to transform children who have heretofore lived their lives in the one world into members of the other. In addition, we assume that the private house or home is a natural institution and that, accordingly, membership in it is a given rather than something one must achieve. Hence we see no reason to prepare people to carry out the tasks and activities associated with it. Perceiving the so-called public world as a human creation and membership in it as something at which one can succeed or fail and therefore as problematic, we make the "real" business of education preparation for carrying out the tasks and activities associated with it.

Granted, the time is long past, if it ever existed, when society was divided into two separate realms or spheres—the public on the one hand, and the private or domestic on the other. Nevertheless, in the United States, as in many other nations, education's societal function is still culturally defined in terms of that opposition. And since schooling is equated with education, so is school's function. Add to this division of society into two worlds the fact that the one has traditionally been considered men's domain and the other one women's, and the culture's way of thinking about education can be seen to be thoroughly gendered. Indeed, one can see that gender is so basic a dimension of education that it permeates our culture's educational ideals, aims, curricula, methodologies, and organizational structures.

Why, for all the end-of-the-20th-century discussion of the ethic of care, is there still a "caring gap" in "high-level" educational discourse? Why does one rarely find the three Cs of care, concern, and connection on those lists of school's goals that public officials periodically draw up? Why are they not on the dockets of teacher training institutions? Why is there no acknowledgment that children need to be protected, no explicit recognition of education for nurturing? Given school's culturally assigned function of equipping children for membership in the world of work, politics, and the professions, these objectives are suspect. It is no exaggeration to say that they might even be deemed dysfunctional. Where, again to use Woolf's terms, possessiveness, jealousy, pugnacity, and greed hold sway, the protection of children will look like mollycoddling (Woolf, 1938). Where adults are expected to be cool and collected and to maintain an emotional distance from others, education in the three Cs of care, concern, and connection is likely to be perceived as a hindrance, not a help.

Woolf told readers of *Three Guineas* that the world of work, politics, and the professions is competitive and that the people there have to be pugnacious and possessive in order to succeed. We in the United States signify our agreement with her by assuming that the qualities or traits of love, nurturance, the overriding values of safety and protection, and the three Cs—all of which are associated with the private home and, hence, with women—run counter to education's raison d'être. Small wonder that the various reports on the condition of American education—reports really about U.S. schools—published in the 1980s and 1990s gave home and the cultural wealth in its keep the silent treatment.

Still, in the United States today almost every child who goes off to school lives in a home as a member of a family of one sort or another and continues to do so as an adult. Yet although as a culture we know that to go beyond life at home is not necessarily to leave that life behind, we nevertheless see school as the place where children cast off the attitudes and values, the patterns of thought and action in the keep of home and domesticity.

As it happens—indeed, as befits school's history—the assets that were historically placed in school's keep represent one small portion of the culture's wealth. When as a result of the Industrial Revolution occupations left the household, school eventually took on the task of preparing young people to enter the workplace—something home gave up doing with work's exodus (Cremin, 1968; Lazerson & Grubb, 1974). School also shouldered what had once been the local community's job of initiating children into the larger society (Cremin, 1965, 1968). Home continued to be held responsible for educating members of the next generation to live there. In turn, school's duty became that of educating them to take their places in the world of politics, work, and the professions.

Serving a different but equally important educational function from home's, school confined itself to transmitting a different but equally important portion of our cultural wealth. Needless to say, since the world of the private home was culturally identified as women's realm and the world of work, politics, and the professions as men's, this division of responsibilities had gendered implications. According to this "logic," school could not be expected to pass down the wealth that had been accumulated by women. Moreover, school was thought to have its hands full trying to pass down to future generations the wealth that had been amassed by men.

And so it was that the historic division between school's and home's responsibilities for transmitting our culture's heritage effectively made school the guardian of a fraction of the wealth. It is, however, downright irrational to assign school a function that is defined in relation to home's educational contributions and at the same time affirm that school is our only educational agent. It is also the height of folly to assign what we take to be our one and only educational agent the one and only task of preparing children for life in the public sphere, when we know full well that they will continue to dwell in private homes as adults. Besides, given the great changes home underwent in the late 20th century, to endorse a function for school that is premised on home's carrying out an opposite but equally important function is short-sighted in the extreme.

Quite simply, the breakdown in the latter part of the 20th century of this culture's gender-based division of labor rendered that old gendered definition of school's function obsolete. The system that denied women entry into the world of work, politics, and the professions had numerous problems, not the least of which was the subordination of women. Nonetheless, if one accepted its premises, it provided a plausible rationale for the way home and school divided up their educational responsibilities. Except in the very poorest families, mothers tended to stay home to do, and to teach their daughters to stay home and do, the domestic work that boys in school relied on as they mastered the knowledge, skills, attitudes, and values required by society's economic and political work. Then things changed. Briefly put, the people culturally assigned responsibility for preserving and transmitting the domestic portion of our cultural wealth became too busy to do this job well. Girls accompanied boys to school, and women from all walks of life entered the public world—which is not to say that the two sexes were treated equally when they got to school or that women were always treated well when they entered the public world.

If society's domestic work were limited to what goes by the name of "housework," it might not matter that the cultural wealth in home's keep is now at risk. But the domestic work to which I refer consists not just of housekeeping but of the emotional and educational labor that in this culture have been major constituents of domesticity. And that includes the adult protection our school director had in mind. Were there a third sex that could be prevailed upon to fill the domestic arena with its presence, act as a mediator between stories and children, and hand down domestic assets such as the three Cs and the ethics of care (see, e.g., Gilligan, 1982; Noddings, 1998) to the next generation, the policy of allowing school to persist in serving its old function might not be misguided. But unless one wants to count the electronic media as such, there is none in the offing. And we all know that the media do far too little to protect children from harm. We all know that, with a few notable exceptions—for instance, *Mr. Rogers' Neighborhood*, *Sesame Street*, *Zoboomafoo*, *Dragon Tales*—the media give scant attention to preserving and transmitting the virtues of care, concern, and connection.

As I write, the nation's public schools are under attack for failing to prepare the next generation adequately. Taking as a given the narrow mission our culture assigns schooling, the critics ignore the palpable fact that the division of labor between school and home on which that mission is premised is now obsolete. They ignore the fact that the narrow mission they assign school belies the monopolistic educational role they give to school. Some would buttress schools through the imposition of state or national standards and perhaps the allotment of funds to repair decaying buildings. Others would give parents a wider choice of schools to which they can send their children, be it through devices such as voucher payments or the establishment of new specially designed schools. No one asks if the wealth that is not in school's keep is elsewhere being transmitted to our young. No one dares talk about what will happen to our young if it is not. Nor does anyone ask what cultural *liabilities* are being passed down to the next generation, let alone calculate the intergenerational injustice the older generation is doing by passing them along.

A NATIONAL CURRICULUM; OR, AN OSTRICHLIKE RESPONSE

An acquaintance who attended elementary school in France once waxed eloquent to a group of friends about the French school system. Tracing in the air the flourishes that he and his classmates had practiced religiously in order to learn to write a fine French hand, he told us how comforting it was to know that every child of his age in the entire country was doing the exact same thing at the very same time. He said it was profoundly reassuring to realize that when the teacher told him to turn to a given page in the textbook, every schoolchild in his grade in all of France was turning to that same page. And in apparent seriousness he suggested that the United States follow France's policy of one curriculum, one set of texts, one time schedule for all.

What gives comfort to one child may distress another, but that is the least of it. Whether Dorothy Sayers's Lord Peter Wimsey was right when he said that "owing to the system of State education in that country, though all the French write vilely, it is rare to find one who writes very much more vilely than the rest" (1934/1962, p. 163), I do not know. Nor in this age of computers is handwriting really the issue. The issue—or, rather, one issue, for it is by no means the only one—is embodied in Sayers's wicked intimation that France's system of total uniformity had yielded mediocrity, or worse.

When I was a fifth-grade teacher, I returned to my class after a brief illness to discover that the school's highly regarded substitute had told my students—and they had believed her—that all the rivers in the world flow from north to south. "Just look at that map hanging on the wall," she reportedly had said to them. "Water flows downhill and, as you can see, south is down." Were howlers like this to be included in a national curriculum, what recourse would children have? Then again, in the early 1970s the third-grade teacher of one of my sons told her class that mainland China, being a communist country, should not under any circumstances be admitted into the United Nations. Here we have not a factual error but a highly controversial and hotly debated topic presented as a matter of settled fact. Were partisanship like this included in a national curriculum, what remedy would there be?

Mind you, in Plato's Just State there would be nothing to remedy. Whatever curriculum his philosopher kings and queens might construct would contain no unwitting falsehoods, no biased political opinions. By definition, the knowledge these men and women acquired by exercising their highly developed powers of reasoning would necessarily be true. To be sure, Plato's rulers are licensed to pass down lies if these are needed to ensure state unity. But notwithstanding this troubling aspect of his philosophy, the fact is that curriculum developers and transmitters in the real world are as fallible as Plato's philosophers are infallible. Thus, even as what the one group thinks true really is true, what the other group thinks true may well be false.

In defense of freedom of thought Mill wrote, "we can never be sure that the opinion we are endeavoring to stifle is a false opinion" (1859/1962,

p. 143). Similarly, we can never be sure that the opinion we are endeavoring to include in a national curriculum is a true opinion. A pluralistic approach to curriculum offers the possibility that mistakes and misrepresentations will be corrected: by other teachers, different texts, or individuals attending other schools. On the other hand, a national curriculum in its extreme form more or less guarantees a long life for errors of fact.

Can't a safety net in the form of feedback from parents and teachers be built into the system? To the extent that they have been subject to the same faulty curriculum, they will be in a poor position to detect the faults.

True, teaching is hard, very hard. If we remove the need for judgment, creativity, and decision making by dictating every move, we greatly simplify the process. But turning teachers into automatons will tend to drive the most intelligent and inspired ones out of the profession. Moreover, automaton teachers are all too likely to fashion their pupils in their own image. And in any case, one can but marvel at the amount of cultural wealth that could be transmitted by school but is necessarily ignored by what is close to being a limiting case of a national curriculum.

Now so far as I am aware, few besides my French-educated friend would have the United States adopt a national curriculum in its most extreme form. But less extreme forms are another matter, especially when they are cleverly disguised. In response to an article appearing in the *New York Times* under the headline "One Education Does Not Fit All" (Reich, 2000), a reader protested that standardized testing "is merely an objective method by which cognitive output can be measured" (Drake, 2000). Would that this modest description did justice to the testing mania that was then possessing the country. In fact, however, the kind of testing at issue serves not merely as a method of measurement but also as a "stand-in" for a national curriculum.

A diverse people who long ago accepted the principle of local control of schooling are understandably reluctant to allow the federal government or even individual state governments to impose one curriculum on all. Represent testing as essential to teacher effectiveness and school accountability, link it to grade promotion and graduation, portray low scores as a national scandal and high scores as a moral victory, and the qualms can be circumvented. Granted, some may doubt the objectivity of the tests. But my point is that whether the test questions are biased or objective, they constitute a selection from certain bodies of knowledge rather than others— for instance, from history rather than music, physics rather than environmental ethics. To answer them, students will therefore have to study those bodies of knowledge and not others. Here and there an intrepid teacher may be able to figure out ways for students to do well on the tests without devoting the entire curriculum to test-related subject matter. Most teachers will be neither so clever, so bold, so devious, nor so devil-may-care. All of which is to say that in the United States at the start of the 21st century, standardized testing functions indirectly to put a national curriculum in place.

According to one commentator, when the United States imported standardized tests, "it did not import the rigorous curriculum that shapes other countries' schools" (Zernike, 2000, p. WK6). Perhaps so. But if the rigor is missing from the attempts to institute a national curriculum in the United States, the existence of the attempts themselves is not in doubt.

Of course, not everyone supports the tests and what they represent. Indeed, a "free school" established in the 1960s experienced record enrollments in 2000 because of the national obsession with testing. Said a founder and staff member, "We can't make peace with the fact that someone thinks they know what everybody should learn, when no one person could possibly encompass all of the useful knowledge in the world" (quoted in Bombardieri, 2000, p. B5).

Advocates of testing ignore the problem of superabundance. In view of how much wealth there is I, however, have difficulty making peace with the fact that the authors of the Massachusetts Comprehensive Assessment System test think everyone should know what part of speech is *hasting* in the line "Until the hasting day has run" (Lehigh, 2000, p. E1). Given that our culture's stock includes liabilities as well as assets, I can make no peace either with the fact that the testing mania deflects attention from the educational problem of generations.

The violence and the shootings; the hate speech and the pornography; the racism, homophobia, and misogyny; the alienation of African American and other minority students; the rampant materialism and the greed; the environmental degradation and the political apathy—the list of cultural liabilities this nation is passing down to its young is long, very long. Nero is said to have fiddled while Rome burned. Well, education's spokespeople can be said to be doing some fiddling of their own. While they debate how best to deliver to the next generation a tiny portion of the culture's assets, a vast cultural debt is being passed down to the culture's young.

My husband and I recently took one of the grandchildren to whom this book is dedicated to a local "child-friendly" restaurant. "This is a mother's heaven. Every city should have one," exclaimed our daughter-in-law as her 19-month-old joined the other toddlers in the well-equipped play area. But even paradise has its perils in a miseducative society. Into this idyllic scene of very young children playing happily with trains, a toy sink, and assorted plastic animals there charged three bigger boys brandishing homemade guns. Making the appropriate noises, they proceeded to mow each other down. No, they did not aim their weapons at the younger children. But in full sight they mimicked over and over again the raids on schools, restaurants, and workplaces that they see on the evening news and the gunfights they watch daily on TV.

The truth is that there is no need for the United States to import a national curriculum from abroad. We already have one. The pressing question for the nation is not "How can we make sure that school transmits the same small portion of cultural wealth to all our young?" but "How can we protect our young from the cultural liabilities that the whole range of our educational agents are transmitting?"

Because of the false equation between education and schooling, it is something of a commonplace to hear what really is a rise in a population's schooling level described as a rise in its level of education. When, however, a public-access cable channel in Connecticut broadcasts White supremacist speeches (Robertson, 2000), a Web site of an independent Baptist Church in Kansas declares "God Hates Fags" (Carnes, 1999, p. 11), and four out of five public school students have experienced sexual harassment in school, the facile equation is suspect. In light of the expanded role of the electronic media in people's lives and the vast array of antisocial and anti-intellectual cultural liabilities these educational agents pass down, it is indeed an enormous leap of faith to suppose that the population is better educated—as opposed simply to receiving more years of schooling—than it used to be.

To increase the nation's level of education, we will have to solve the problem of cultural miseducation. That the problem's solution depends on an acknowledgment of the multiplicity of educational agency and the admission that school has custody of only a small portion of our culture's wealth bears repeating. So does the fact that it also depends on our recognizing that our culture's stock contains liabilities as well as assets.

I spoke earlier of the need to put a halt to our collective squandering of the culture's wealth. Seeing no signs of an invisible hand working in the public interest, I gave this task to education in the broadest sense of that term. Let me repeat how vital it is to distribute across the entire population an impulse to preserve and transmit the wealth. And let me add that it is equally vital to distribute to everyone the desire and the will to staunch the flow of liabilities from one generation to the next.

CHAPTER 4

Minimizing the Liabilities

CULTURAL BOOKKEEPING; OR, THE CULTURAL-WEALTH RESEARCH PROJECT

When a friend learned that I had just received a small grant from the Spencer Foundation to record the educational memories of my elementary school classmates, she expressed surprise that such a project had been funded. Once I explained that we had been part of that great American experiment known as progressive education, she said in amazement: "Do you mean to say that you went to a school like the Little Red School House in New York City?" "The very one," I replied. "Well, Jane," she said after a long pause. "Now I understand the work in the philosophy of education you have been doing all these years!"

Whether the distinctive nature of that school experience sheds as much light on my philosophical research as this woman implied I do not know. The older I get, however, the more convinced I am that my early schooling did have a profound effect on my educational thinking. It is no accident that one theme this "product" of a Deweyan education has repeatedly stressed in her own research and writing is that both general and liberal education, as these are defined by our culture, are overly narrow and intellectualistic. It is no mere happenstance that a major premise of all my work is that an adequate alternative to the received idea of an educated person as a disembodied mind will have to unite mind and body, thought and action, reason and emotion.

Although my present preoccupation with the wealth of cultures has taken me in directions Dewey chose not to travel, it, too, connects to my early schooling. As 8-year-olds, my class built a teepee and enacted some of the activities of American Indian life. As 10-year-olds, we were ancient Egyptians and their Hebrew slaves; for years afterward, I delighted in having been one of the Egyptian bearers who carried a dead Pharaoh onto the school stage, where we proceeded to wrap our classmate up tightly as a mummy. For many years I was also proud of having played the part of a Hebrew slave compelled to make bricks without straw. Switching identities in true postmodern fashion, at age 11 my friends and I became medieval serfs, after which we wrote and produced a play based on the life of Harriet Tubman. Then as 12-year-olds, we were colonial Americans. And all the while we went on walks around Greenwich Village, took trips to the Harlem Art Center and the Egyptian wing of the Metropolitan Museum, studied immigrant groups, and sang songs of other cultures.

From our immersion in other times and peoples, we children became vicariously acquainted with a wide range of cultural assets and liabilities. Even as we learned to value the one sort, we came to abhor the other. Yet I know from my own experience that one can learn to value or appreciate a portion of one's own or another culture's wealth without developing a direct impulse to preserve it, let alone a desire to preserve the wealth of cultures more generally. By sending us into Catskill Mountain communities to collect songs, stories, and artifacts, my summer camp did bequeath the desire to preserve such wealth. We did not collect the songs because we already had that desire: The collecting produced the desire. But in my own case at least, the impulse to preserve a particular portion of cultural wealth did not automatically translate into a more general interest in preservation. Nor did it necessarily persuade my campmates and me to do what we could to block the miseducative tendencies of our own society.

Children need to be taught not only to value their culture's assets but also to guard against its liabilities. Most children in the United States know the value of economic wealth from an early age. Practically every educational agent gives instruction in this to adults and children alike. Teaching that cultural wealth is as important as economic wealth and that cultural liabilities can be as dangerous as economic ones is another matter altogether.

I have already said that, in view of the dispersion of educational agency throughout contemporary society, one vital step toward the solution to the educational problem of generations is the acknowledgment by the whole range of educational agents that they are both guardians and transmitters of our culture's stock. It would be a fatal mistake, however, to rely purely on the good intentions of educational agents who, after "seeing the light," embrace the ideal of an educative society. Some agents may never see the light. In response to a report that the television industry has failed to keep its word to attach rating labels to its programs, a children's TV activist said, "Anybody who thought the broadcast industry was going to rate some of their nonsense so it would be meaningful to parents must be living on another planet" (Aucoin, 1998, p. A14). Moreover, the hoped-for maturity will not in any case occur overnight. And supposing it were to, even the most mature educational agents are fallible. Thus, another vital step toward solving the educational problem of generations is the reduction of the power the stories have over children and adults. For if the sensibilities of the grownups in a child's life have been hardened by the stories heard at the workplace, in the neighborhood, or on the media, how will they be able to act as responsible mediators?

There is much talk today about the importance of teaching young people to think critically, but rarely, if ever, is it suggested that this kind of thinking be harnessed to the goal of creating an educative society. Yet a society that rejects Plato's program of censorship—as an open, democratic society must—has little choice. We can let the cultural liabilities get the best of our progeny and us. Or we can proceed with the business of solving the educational problem of generations by seeing that men, women, and children become acutely conscious of the many miseducative agents in our midst; by figuring out how to defuse and deconstruct for ourselves and each other the potentially dangerous messages they send; and, above all, by instilling in all members of the culture the desire to make this miseducative society a genuinely educative one.

For a spirit of cooperation to prevail among the multitude of education's agents, there will have to be some way of determining how each one's curriculum—hidden or otherwise—relates to the curricula of other agents. Thus, another vital step in solving the educational problem of generations is the establishment of a system of "cultural bookkeeping" whose object is to keep track of the culture's wealth and liabilities and to develop full-blown portraits of its educational agents. I say "a" system, but just as there are alternative ways to keep a business's books, there can be different methods of cultural bookkeeping. Providing an overview of the culture's stock—the holdings, the guardians, the transmission mechanisms, the distribution patterns, and so on—one or several bookkeeping systems would allow a realistic appraisal of the educational problem of generations and provide the database needed for responsible decision making.

It goes without saying that a satisfactory cultural bookkeeping system presupposes a vast amount of research. The "cultural-wealth research project" I envision would seek first of all to identify the culture's educational agents and its stock. Assets and liabilities would then have to be distinguished and an inventory of each agent's stock taken. Of course, the location of that stock on its custodian's preservation continuum would have to be determined, as would each educational agent's transmission mechanisms. In addition, it would be vital to know to which segments of the population the stock has been transferred.

At a 1998 concert of popular songs composed from the 1890s through the 1930s, the pianist sought to impress upon his audience how much things had changed during his own performing career. Just 30 years ago he had never heard of Scott Joplin and tonight he was playing two rags familiar to everyone in the hall. Here, the issue is not the location of Joplin's music on its guardians' preservation continua or the way it was transmitted to future generations. The issue is the population to whom the wealth was being distributed. I hazard the guess that most people in that almost entirely white audience were in the same position of ignorance 30 years ago as the pianist himself, but this scarcely means that nobody in the United States knew Joplin's name or was familiar with his music.

Overgeneralizing from the data at hand is a trap that our cultural-wealth research project had best avoid. That Joplin's music was not being passed down to the classical music community in 1968—a community that was predominantly white and middle class—is in itself no indication that this wealth was not passed down to anybody. To determine just who in fact were or are the inheritors of a given portion of a culture's assets and liabilities, one must again look and see.

Should a particular item of stock be moved to a different point on its guardian's preservation continuum? Should a different educational agent be assigned custody of it? Should it be distributed to a broader or perhaps a narrower segment of the next generation? A broad-based cultural-wealth research project would allow questions like these to be answered.

This vast research effort would of necessity be ongoing, for in a changing world the cultural balance sheet is constantly shifting. The inquiries would also be interdisciplinary.

Imagine, then, a cultural-wealth research project that encompasses the following:

Historical research on the lives and times of the various educational agents and portions of cultural stock

Philosophical analyses of key concepts, such as "living legacy," "preservation," "educational agent," and the "wealth–liability" distinction

Normative work on, for instance, what cultural stock should be preserved as living legacy or dead relic and what the various distribution patterns should be

Social science research on, among other things, the workings of the various educational agents, cultural definitions of cultural wealth, and the actual as opposed to the intended distribution pattern for some portion of stock

Depicting the life and times of a Van Gogh masterpiece from its creation in 1890 to its sale in 1990 for $82.5 million, what was then the highest price to be paid at an auction for a work of art, Cynthia Saltzman's (1998) *Portrait of Dr. Gachet* is a wonderful example of one of the many kinds of research a good bookkeeping system would require. A narrative of how an item of cultural stock not only acquired economic value and cultural esteem but became a living legacy, Saltzman's book is also a case study of how differently the same item of wealth can fare in the custody of different guardians. By including in her discussion interpretative materials about the portrait, critical assessments of it, biographical information about Van Gogh, and historical information about the times, Saltzman also offers insight of a theoretical kind into the nature of cultural objects or stock. It is her book that led me to formulate the hypothesis that a cultural object—be it an artifact, idea, event, human practice, or what have you—acts as a "magnet." It pulls together other items of stock—themselves cultural objects in their own right.

A very different example of research into the life and times of a single item of cultural stock was published in the *New York Times* (Blair & Weissman, 2000). "The Biography of a Gun" tells the story of one 12-shot, 9-millimeter Jennings semiautomatic from its manufacture in California to its use in 13 crimes, including several murders, and eventually to its recovery by the police. The tale may not be morally uplifting, but it illustrates the importance of including the tracking of liabilities in a system of cultural bookkeeping.

Bowling Alone, Robert Putnam's (2000) important inquiry into the growth and decline of America's social capital, represents yet another kind of study of the life and times of a portion of cultural stock. In fact, because Putnam views associations large and small, formal and informal as capital, this book also serves as one model of inquiry into our culture's educational agents. To document the decline of civic engagement in the latter part of the 20th century, Putnam first reviews an enormous body of social scientific evidence showing how the nation's voluntary associations have changed over time. He then follows the career of some of the personal traits or virtues that also come under the heading of social capital—among them altruism, social trust, volunteerism, political participation, and reciprocity. One of the things that makes his study particularly relevant to a cultural bookkeeping project is that he traces changes in the distribution patterns of these virtues over time and across the general population. Another is that although in the cultural arena quantification of the kind associated with bookkeeping in the literal sense is not possible, statistical research is nonetheless important.

An excellent example of another kind of research required by a system of cultural bookkeeping can be found in *A Tradition That Has No Name* by Mary Belenky, Lynne Bond, and Jacqueline Weinstock (1996). In Part 3 of that book, Belenky describes her study of four "Public Homeplaces," two in Germany and two in the United States. These organizations are founded and led by women whose primary mission is to bring marginalized people "to voice" (1996, p. 156). Although Belenky goes out of her way to call them "noneducational" institutions (p. 161), from a cultural-wealth perspective they definitely qualify as educational agents. Indeed, Belenky herself asked what enabled the founders of these organizations to establish "such highly collaborative and creative learning environments" (p. 157).

After visiting these Public Homeplaces "to see how their ideas were being played out in action" (pp. 158–159), interviewing the founders, attending staff meetings, and conducting group interviews with members of the four organizations, Belenky was able to provide a detailed account of each one's history, structure, and goals. Belenky also identified a vitally important, too often ignored item of wealth over which these four agents have joint custody. She alternately calls this cultural asset "practices that sponsor the development of people who, in turn, go on to make their families and communities more nurturing places for others" (p. 159), "the goal of elevating the whole community" (p. 160), "the developmental tradition" (p. 169), a tradition of "leadership oriented to development" (p. 174), and "a tradition that has no name" (p. 176).

Theresa Funiciello's (1993) *Tyranny of Kindness* presents a very different sort of portrait of an educational agent—in this case the New York City and State welfare systems. Whereas *A Tradition That Has No Name* depicts Public Homeplaces as the preservers and transmitters of especially valuable cultural assets, *Tyranny of Kindness* portrays a welfare system that passes down devastating cultural liabilities. By no means does Funiciello confine her indictment of the welfare system to an analysis of its dehumanization and demonizing of the poor. Even as her book tells us what the system teaches poor people and everyone else about poor people and poverty, it documents what damage the system does to poor people in particular and to society in general. It also tells the story of the Downtown Welfare Advocate Center— an organization that seems to fit Belenky's description of a Public Homeplace. But Funiciello's exposé of the educational aspect of the welfare system is especially pertinent here: It demonstrates how important it is for a cultural bookkeeping project to identify and track the activities of the culture's miseducators as well as its educators.

Inventories represent another kind of research on which a system of cultural bookkeeping must rely. One notable example of this genre is *The Dictionary of Global Culture* edited by Kwame Anthony Appiah and Henry Louis Gates, Jr. (1996). In their introduction, the editors explain that their object is to give people in the West who are aware of their ignorance of other traditions and want to know more "a sampler of cultural contributions from around the globe" (p. xi). Nowhere do they mention the earlier inventory compiled by Hirsch and his colleagues, but the subtitle "From Diderot to Bo Diddley—What Every American Needs to Know as We Enter the Next Century" gives notice that this volume is meant to be a corrective to *The Dictionary of Cultural Literacy*.

Beginning with *Abakwa, Sociedab*, "a secret society of African extraction based in Cuba," and ending with *zudeco*, "a style of country-dance music descended from Cajun, Afro-Caribbean, and Afro-American traditions," the global dictionary itemizes a huge amount of the world's cultural stock, portions of which the editors of the earlier venture may not have known about. Even so, as the editors themselves make clear, this compilation is far from complete. The project began when Appiah and Gates asked a Chinese colleague to list "a few products of Chinese civilization that, in her opinion, all educated people should know" (1996, pp. xi–xii). To their great surprise, her list differed significantly from the one they had expected her to submit. Next they invited academics around the world to suggest 50 "of the most important cultural contributions from the region in which they were expert" (p. xii)—and the rest is history.

Another spectacular example of inventory taking is Diana Eck's Pluralism Project (1996). It got its start in 1991 when Eck's Harvard research seminar visited Islamic mosques, a Sri Lakshmi temple, Hindu communities, Sikh gurdwaras, a Jain temple, and Buddhist meditation centers—all of them in Boston and its environs. The Pluralism Project then sent multiethnic and -religious research teams of college students across the United States for three successive summers. In cultural-wealth terms, their job was to identify and locate as many custodians as they could of that portion of religious stock that fell outside the standard U.S. categories of Protestant, Catholic, or Jewish. In addition to mosques, temples, and the like, the guardians of this "new" wealth included newspapers, magazines, feminist Zen sitting groups, and more. Besides counting how many such agents then existed in the United States and where they were located, the project sought to trace the changes that had occurred in the "foreign" stock because of the "American experience"; the emergence of brand-new wealth, such as ecumenical Buddhism; the transmission of cultural liabilities pertaining to the new "foreign" wealth, such as violence directed at minority religions; and the development of patterns of cooperation between and among educational agents (Eck, 1996).

Whereas Eck dispatched Harvard students across the country to identify the preservers and transmitters of one type of cultural stock, Gerald

Grant sent Syracuse University graduate students into a single metropolitan area to study its educational system, broadly defined. Rejecting the false equation between education and schooling, Grant's researchers focused their attention on local newspapers, museums in the area, rap music videos, local literacy programs, civic associations, adolescent support networks, community-based mediation programs, local health information disseminators, an agency called Transitions, Inc., which provided unemployed managers and professionals with counseling, technological assistance, office space, and much more. After reporting their results to the university and the community at a daylong conference, the group published its findings in a project report, *The Educational Life of the Community: Outcomes of a Metropolitan Study* (Grant, 1996).

I am well aware that even when cultural bookkeeping is restricted to a single locality it is an enormous undertaking. Expand the context to a region, a nation, a continent, the globe and a cultural bookkeeping system together with the research project it presupposes sound wildly ambitious. But so did the publicly funded human genome project, whose goal was to decipher all 3.2 billion chemical letters of the human genetic blueprint, when it was launched in 1990.

I also fully understand the fear that too much knowledge can be a dangerous thing in that Big Brother can use it to tighten his control over the populace. One commentator has said that what is frightening about George Orwell's *1984* is not just its representation of political oppression. "Less terrifying but alarming enough is the vision of the penetration of state monitoring, and hence state power, into every recess of private life" (Rule, 1983, p. 167). Who would disagree? However, the domain of cultural bookkeeping includes the culture's assets, liabilities, and educational agents—not the behavior and lives of individuals. Of course, knowledge, like power, can always be abused. And it might even be the case that the more knowledge we have, the greater the abuses can be. But the truth is that the kind of knowledge that feeds Big Brother's appetite to control the private actions of an entire population, or else some segment thereof, is increasingly available and is not at all the result of cultural bookkeeping. Just think of observation satellites that, while orbiting more than 400 miles above Earth, can distinguish not just roads and bridges but cars, homes, and even hot tubs (Harvey, 2001). Indeed, by tracking the decline of cultural assets such as civic engagement and documenting the increased distribution of such liabilities as political inertia and acquiescence to authority, a system of cultural bookkeeping could serve to thwart Big Brother's totalitarian impulses.

And finally consider this: If a system of tracking is developed, our culture will be in a position to decide which portions of its wealth are at risk. For those at risk, it will be in a position to decide which portions should be put in the custody of different agents. It will be able to determine whether some of the items presently at risk might replace cultural liabilities now being transmitted as living legacies and whether these latter could be moved to a different position on the relevant educational agent's preservation continuum. In other words, we will be in a position to solve the educational problem of generations.

PROTECTION AND CENSORSHIP; OR, A CULTURAL-WEALTH CURRICULUM FOR SCHOOL AND SOCIETY

In the introduction to a 1981 reprint of *Weather in the Streets*—itself a blessed instance of cultural preservation—Janet Watts reported that its author, Rosamond Lehmann, could no longer remember whether in writing her earlier novel, *Invitation to the Waltz*, she already had a sequel in mind. "But when I came to the meeting between Olivia [the young heroine of *Invitation to the Waltz*] and Rollo on the terrace," Lehmann told her, "I think I thought; I see! *this* is what all this is about! It's unrealised now, it's broken off—but this is what I've got to deal with later" (Watts, 1981, np). And so she did—in *Weather in the Streets*.

From the vantage point of 10 rather than 50 years, I can say with some assurance that when *The Schoolhome* (Martin, 1992) was published, I did not already have a sequel in mind. Yet I now see that the cultural-wealth perspective I am formulating in this book is what *The Schoolhome* was all about.

When I wrote *The Schoolhome*, I had not yet developed my concept of cultural wealth. Nonetheless, that book can be read as a treatise on the subject. My overriding concern in *The Schoolhome*—or, to put it more starkly, the fear that impelled me to write as I did there—was that the values, the virtues, the ways of thinking, the patterns of acting, and the modes of being that are associated in U.S. culture with home and domesticity were at risk of disappearing. And although I had not yet developed the idea of multiple educational agency that is so central to a cultural-wealth perspective, *The Schoolhome* presupposed this very concept. It is part of the book's main thesis that home and school are partners in the education of our nation's young. I adopted that perspective because due to changes in home and family in the last decades of the 20th century, home could no longer carry out the educational functions this partnership took for granted.

At the heart of *The Schoolhome* is the proposal that school step into the breach created by the great social transformations of the late 20th century and start serving as a "moral equivalent of home." Hence my recommendation that we turn our school*houses* into school*homes*—places where the three Cs of care, concern, and connection hold sway. Ten years after that book's publication, I have had to ask myself what becomes of the idea of a schoolhome when one adopts a cultural-wealth framework. Lehmann's heroine in *Invitation to the Waltz* was a sensitive, but basically carefree, teenager. By the time Olivia reappeared in *Weather in the Streets*, she was a divorced woman at loose ends: quite as sympathetic a character, but greatly changed. Does the idea of a schoolhome change when it is incorporated into a cultural-wealth perspective? Is it perhaps rendered superfluous by an approach to education that stresses multiple educational agency? Although in these pages I have been assuming school's continued existence, this is not an idle question. Once school's monopolistic hold over education is broken, it is fair to ask what place, if any, it deserves in the educational firmament.

Illich's (1972) *Deschooling Society* can be read as an answer to this question—or, rather, as giving two quite different answers, since Illich's proposal to deschool society admits of two very different interpretations. According to one common rendering of *Deschooling Society*, Illich was recommending that we end school's monopoly over education and recognize instead that school is but one among many of the culture's educational agents. According to another far more radical reading, Illich was proposing to dispense with schools altogether: to dismantle, abolish, eradicate not just our nation's established school system but each and every school there is now or might some day be.

Now by no stretch of the imagination does a cultural-wealth approach to education cancel out society's need for a moral equivalent of home. When Illich wrote his book, his concern was the false equation of education with one of its forms, schooling. In 1972 he was not worried about the coming changes in home and family that would soon create a huge domestic vacuum in children's lives. How could he have been? Nor was he thinking about the violence that just two decades later led me to develop the idea of a schoolhome. Has the violence been eradicated in the years since I first formulated this new concept of school? On the contrary, children today have readier access to guns, drugs, hate speech, and pornographic excesses than ever. Today, one must add electronic harassment to the violence at home and in the world. Today, there are death threats on the Internet and shootings in the schools Illich was criticizing.

Nonetheless, however great the need for a moral equivalent of home, it does not follow as night the day that school should step into the breach. Granted that the domestic vacuum and the violence have by now become all too ordinary facts of children's lives, it is perfectly possible to abandon the very idea of school, as many readers understood Illich to have been doing, and single out another educational agent to serve as home's moral equivalent.

I readily acknowledge that, from a strictly logical point of view, school has no claim on us. At risk of sounding irredeemably old-fashioned, let me say, however, that school for all its faults still strikes me as the best qualified of our culture's educational agents to fill the domestic vacuum and reduce the violence. After all, this is the place where almost every child spends many hours a day. And there is yet another reason why we should consider school as one among many educational agents and not abolish it altogether: School can take its place in the vanguard of the movement to transform this miseducative society into an educative one.

To opt for school is not to take a stand on such thorny issues as school choice, voucher systems, and the like. Nor in asking school to stanch the flow of liabilities to the next generation do I absolve society's other educational agents from doing the same. Illich condemned school's hidden curriculum for passing down undesirable traits, attitudes, worldviews, and the like—in other words, for transmitting cultural liabilities to the next generation. One does not have to dispute this assessment to acknowledge that the nonschool educational agents of society whose praises Illich sang were doing just this. Because he ignored the fact that the whole wide range of society's groups and institutions have hidden curricula, Illich overlooked the educational problem of generations. A cultural-wealth approach to education cannot afford this luxury. Nor can a society that aspires to being educative allow vast numbers of its educational agents to engage in miseducation.

Years ago in discussing what to do with a hidden curriculum when you find one, I proposed that school make children aware of the hidden agenda of the culture's nonschool educators (Martin, 1994, ch. 8). A program of consciousness raising is what I called for on the grounds that people who know what is going on are in a better position to resist what is being foisted upon them. I located this program in school for the same reason that, when writing *The Schoolhome*, I singled out school to fill the domestic vacuum in children's lives: We can be fairly sure of finding the nation's children there. Think of a program for raising children's consciousness about the cultural liabilities being passed down to them as part of a cultural-wealth curriculum and both school and program take on an added dimension

One typical response to stories that are perceived as potentially harmful to children and adolescents is to ban them from classrooms. "The repeated use of the word 'nigger' in *Huckleberry Finn* hurts my daughter," said a highly articulate woman on my television screen the other evening. "She should not be made to read that book in school," she added. As if in answer, the author of *Responding to Hate at School* writes:

Remember that some "classics" and mainstream literary works contain language, scenes and characters that may offend some students. The novel *Huckleberry Finn*, for example, has raised widespread concerns over its use of the word "nigger." Before assigning such a book, discuss with students the objectionable elements and their possible interpretations, and communicate with parents about your reasons for using the material. Avoid singling out members of minority groups in the process. Keep in mind that the appropriateness of such materials is always subject to debate. (Carnes, 1999, p. 12)

Unless the offending stories are banned from the larger society as Socrates advised, a strategy of silence in school gets things backward. When stories are read or heard or seen in school, the teacher can act as mediator between text and child, and so deflect the harm that would otherwise be done. In the outside world a direct, unmediated, two-way relation between story and audience is the rule. So long as the world outside school is filled with stories that cause children pain in the short run and in the longer run transmit the culture's liabilities, silence in school is an unacceptable course of action. That U.S. culture is filled with stories that hurt African Americans was pointed out by everyone else on this television program.

A colleague told me that when she was a high school English teacher, her principal questioned her assigning Willa Cather's *My Antonia* to her classes because Antonia's father commits suicide in the novel. But the Socratic worry that impressionable teenage readers of the book will be unduly upset by or regard with favor or possibly even try to emulate the father's action ignores the teacher's role as mediator between story and audience. If the father's suicide in *My Antonia* is potentially injurious to teenagers—and I do not for a moment say that it is—how much better for them to read the book with someone who can calm fears even as she raises the issue of suicide and alternative courses of action for discussion. How much better to read the oft-banned *Huckleberry Finn* in a classroom in which a teacher, acting as intermediary between the book's racist language and her students, can talk about Mark Twain's realism, connect his characters' speech patterns to America's racism, and explore the way what is now called hate speech makes its targets feel (cf. Carnes, 1999, p. 15). How much better for Jewish and non-Jewish students alike to encounter Shakespeare's controversial portrayal of Shylock in *The Merchant of Venice* in a setting in which a teacher explains and encourages discussion of the apparently anti-Semitic tenor of the text. How much better for school to act as a mediator between the children in its care and the stories of the world.

What counts as good mediation between child and text? Would that a cultural-wealth perspective on education came with ready-made lesson plans about what to do in a second- or sixth- or ninth-grade classroom next Tuesday! But the suggestions I make in this chapter are not blueprints for action.

To suggest that they could or should be is to suppose that the questions at issue can be decided in the abstract. They cannot be. Thus, as Mill in *On Liberty* offered not so much applications of his two principles of liberty as "specimens of application" (1859/1962, p. 226), I attach "application sketches" to my cultural-wealth perspective. These are to be filled in and, if necessary, redrawn as the exigencies of educational practice and the ever-changing character of the problem of cultural miseducation dictate.

In the present instance, what qualifies as good mediation will depend on both child and story—*My Antonia* and *Huckleberry Finn* will require very different kinds of teacher interventions. It will also depend on whether the object is the protection of children from injury "here and now" or in the future. Both aims are crucial, yet they may call for quite different responses. Here and now, or "on the spot," protection may sometimes require nothing more than a teacher saying, "These are not the author's views. He is putting the words in his character's mouth in order to show how wrong the view actually is." To protect African American children against *future* injury from racist language of the sort found in *Huckleberry Finn* or Jewish children from the stereotypes and prejudices represented in *The Merchant of Venice* is quite another matter.

I am not saying that future protection can ever be fully guaranteed. Some years ago a tenured professor at my university told me that upon arriving at his university office that morning he had found a virulent homophobic message scrawled on the door. Although he himself was an expert in the field of gay and lesbian studies and knew just about all there was to know about homophobia, he was in a state of shock. Yet even if the promise of total protection from future injury is illusory, knowledge of what is happening and why can make a difference—and so can a willingness to question the behavior of the culture's educational agents. I therefore envision a "cultural-wealth curriculum" that would ideally be adopted by all of education's agents. Its first phase would be the consciousness raising I have been describing. A second phase would be to give young people an understanding of the racism, anti-Semitism, homophobia, and misogyny they experience. And a third would be to encourage them to undertake cultural-wealth research projects of their own.

Which of our educational agents are actually transmitting the hate speech one hears in school, on the streets, at sports events? What transmission mechanisms are being used? Even very young children can learn how to monitor the television programs they watch, the electronic games they play, and the Web sites they visit. They can keep daily logs of how and when and in what form cultural liabilities are being preserved and passed down and can try to trace the life and times of the offending stock. Having done this much and then pooled their findings, they are in a good position to learn how to deconstruct for themselves the potentially harmful stories they encounter in the outside world.

Would that the world's stories were no more harmful than *My Antonia*, *Huckleberry Finn*, and *The Merchant of Venice*! But there is hard-core pornography; Nazi depictions of Jews as rodents; long lists on the Internet of nigger jokes, Jew jokes, and faggot jokes; and a lot more besides. Although I say that it is far better to read potentially injurious materials in school where they can be mediated than on the outside, it is necessary to ask whether some stories are so vicious, so virulent that it would be a travesty on education to bring them into classrooms.

I do not believe that hard-core pornography should be shown to 5-year-olds. In fact, I do not believe that either it or the Nazi depictions of Jews or jokes that reduce African Americans to animals should exist. But they do, and they are available to all who have the desire and the patience to search the Internet. To my mind, therefore, the question is not *whether* school should maintain its present policy of silence about the world's worst stories. Given their availability to children of all ages, given the reluctance of the culture's other educational agents to regulate them, and given the enormous power of the messages at issue to do serious injury to young and old alike, the question is *how best* to bring the study of them into the next generation's curriculum proper so as to dilute their potential to do future harm.

Let me make it very clear that children can learn how to deconstruct different types of stories so that their potential for doing harm is diluted without being shown the most brutal and disturbing examples of them. Whether at some point in young people's development it is appropriate for them to see these latter materials is a difficult question that demands more attention than I can give it here. My own personal feeling is that no child—or, for that matter adult—should be compelled to look at hard-core pornographic or racist materials. On the other hand, because so many of those who minimize the power of these stories to do injury seem never to have seen—or else, never to have looked closely at—hard-core examples, I also feel strongly that those lacking firsthand acquaintance with these materials should not take it upon themselves to defend them.

One vital question posed by the existence of hard-core pornography and hate literature is whether, in the name of the responsible protection of children, these should be brought into classrooms. The closely related phenomenon of hate speech poses no such dilemma: Like pornography, it regularly occurs both in school and on the outside.

Legal theorists struggle with the problem that hate speech poses the First Amendment to the Constitution. Should it or should it not be protected from governmental regulation? Can it or can it not legitimately be banned when it occurs on college and university campuses? Some would shield hate speech at all costs. Pointing to the injuries done by the speech, some seek ways to punish offenders without violating the Bill of Rights. But hate speech is not just a legal or quasi-legal issue. As the magazine *Teaching Tolerance* recognized when it published a guide for teachers, counselors, and administrators, it is also an educational issue.

I find it hard to believe that whoever wrote on a University of Michigan blackboard "A mind is a terrible thing to waste—especially on a nigger" (Matsuda, Lawrence, Delgado, & Crenshaw, 1993, p. 55) had suddenly resorted to hate speech after having employed race-friendly language all his or her life. It is difficult for me to imagine that the person who scratched "Death Nigger" on a counselor's door at Purdue University had not learned the language of hate long before. No one is born a racist or misogynist. These cultural liabilities are passed down by a host of educational agents when children are very young.

The year is 1989. Sixth-graders in a Boston area public school are asked to tell the first word that comes to mind about the other sex. The girls say: "Fine. Jerks. Conceited. Ugly. Crazy. Dressy. Sexy. Dirty minds. Boring. Rude. Cute. Stuck up. Desperate. Sexually abusive. Punks." The boys say: "Pumping ('big tits'). Nasty. Vagina. Dope bodies (big breasts and behinds). Door knob (breasts). Hooker. Skeezer ('a girl who will "do it" with 50 guys')" (Jackson, 1989, p. 23).

The scene switches to Australia. It is still 1989 and primary school girls are speaking:

> There's a group of boys in our class who always tease us and call us—you know, dogs, aids, slut, moll and that.

> This boy used to call us big-tits and period-bag and used to punch us in the breasts.

> They call us rabies, dogs, aids.

> They reckon I'm a dog. My brother gave me to them. He said, "Oh, come here, I've got a pet for you. Do you want my dog?" And he gave me to them as a pet dog. (Clark, 1989, pp. 25, 39, 40)

Now it is the spring of 1997 and a teacher in the western part of the United States writes me a letter:

> Dear Jane,
> I love teaching and seem to understand middle school kids. I teach in a rural town. . . . I find myself talking to kids about their homophobic/racist/sexist language more than I'd like to believe.

> There are a few boys in each class who become so angry with me
> whenever I bring up women in a positive way. For example, I asked
> all my classes to do a quick-write about important women in their
> lives before International Women's Day. More than a few boys
> wrote "Women suck. Men rule!"

Who exactly transmits hate language and, with it, the attitudes it expresses? Educational agents ranging from home, family, church, community, peer groups, and the welfare system to the print and electronic media and the Internet. I wish I could say that schools and universities do not contribute to the transmission process. However, in a 1999 survey, teachers reported that they hear biased comments more often from colleagues than from students (Carnes, 1999, p. 17). And supposing teachers refrain from using biased language, to the extent that they ignore racist, misogynist, anti-Semitic, homophobic, and other forms of hate speech when it occurs in their environs, or blame its use on the victims, or treat it as a problem of law enforcement only, they are complicit in the process.

In 1997 a girl attending a New England prep school found a virulent anti-Semitic note on her dresser. More notes followed over a 2-month period, as did a swastika and a message in the shower saying, "Gas for the Jew." One year later the school paid her a settlement and issued an apology rather than suffer a lawsuit. It seems that the school had called in the police and had given the girl a lie detector test. It had also, without the evidence to support its claim, sent a letter to parents implying that the target of the hate language was also its perpetrator (Zernike & Sargent, 1998).

Regarding hate speech as a legal issue involving questions of crime and punishment, the school abdicated its educational responsibilities. Focusing exclusively on who was to blame, it did not think to teach its students the moral, political, and social meaning of the anti-Semitic messages—no matter who the author of them might have been. The Australian girl who reported that the boys in her class call the girls "dogs, aids, slut," and so forth, said: "There's no point telling teachers 'cos they just say 'they're just teasing', or 'they didn't hurt you'! You feel like you're wasting your time" (Clark, 1989, p. 25). Teacher silence regarding hate language—not to mention teacher use of same—sends the wrong messages to victims and perpetrators alike. The latter learn that in adult eyes their behavior is perfectly acceptable. The former learn to suffer in silence (cf Carnes, 1999, p. 17).

Legal scholars list some of the injuries that hate speech produces. Causing immediate emotional distress and long-term emotional pain, and creating self-doubt and self-hatred, it tends to silence its victims. Damaging the reputation of its targets, it causes others to take "those people" less seriously while encouraging the victims to internalize the devaluation of themselves (Matsuda et al., 1993). If hate speech rarely occurred in school, the tendency of teachers to mask its racist or misogynist content by, for example, calling it teasing or saying "boys will be boys" might not matter. Or rather, their silence on the subject might not be so significant if the speech occurred infrequently, or never, in the world outside school. But observers assure us that at least some forms of hate speech are staples of all too many school environments. Furthermore, in a society in which hate speech is rampant, even a single occurrence of it in school is an occasion of considerable import.

On the most basic level, in-school hate speech forces teachers and staff to choose: Do we protect those children who are its targets here and now or do we not? Given the harm that face-to-face hate speech does its targets, to opt for nonprotection is to allow the injuries. Suppose that a racial epithet is used in a classroom, is painted on bathroom walls, or is shouted across a playground or dormitory quadrangle. School or university officials can ignore it, but in so doing they fail to protect the affected parties from immediate injury. The perpetrators can be chastised or punished, but disciplinary action still does not mitigate the injury the victims suffer here and now. Moreover, although one standard justification for punishment is that it serves as a deterrent, the fact that it so often fails in this function warrants our asking whether punishment without specific education for prevention will bar future occurrences of hate speech in school. And supposing it does, one may wonder whether it will really discourage the in-school perpetrators from indulging in the practice of hate speech in society at large or deter school's nonperpetrators from indulging in the practice on the outside.

In between the two extremes of school censorship of hate speech and school callousness to harm stands a third option: Teachers and staff can act as mediators between children and story when hate speech occurs and can also put in place a cultural-wealth curriculum in which the students become their own cultural bookkeepers. This is the option I recommend, and I propose that it also be embraced by the culture's other educational agents. In one situation this course of action may initially involve physically interposing oneself between Caucasian and African American or between boy and girl and symbolically taking the injury into one's own body and soul. In another it may mean turning to the target of the epithet, looking into her eyes, and telling her that she is not a dog or a slut; she is a wonderful, beautiful, intelligent human being who should feel very proud of being a girl. The actions teachers or representatives of nonschool agents take will ultimately depend on the immediate context. Because of the power of hate speech to injure here and now, it is imperative, however, that it be mediated at the time it occurs or as soon thereafter as possible—even if this means interrupting something as sacrosanct as a math class, an examination, or a competitive sporting event.

It is tempting to call the kind of mediation whose sole object is protection against injury here and now "passive" or "negative." These labels are misleading, however, for even the simplest mediation requires positive action. Thinking back on my own schooling, I find it hard to imagine that my classmates and I used hate language. For one thing, our curriculum incorporated what would now be called African American studies. For another, the school's prevailing ethos was profoundly antiracist. Nonetheless, protective mediation did occur. I, for one, vividly recall the day in eighth grade when a boy who often made us laugh leaned so far back in his chair that he fell over. Of course he had done it on purpose, of course the rest of us roared with appreciation, and of course the teacher sent him out of the room. Then, to our great surprise and eventual shame, she read us the riot act. "Don't you know that what you were doing was racist? Don't you see that the reason he is always clowning is that he thinks it is the only way he will be liked? Don't you care that by laughing at his antics you are promoting the stereotype of the happy-go-lucky Negro? Don't let me ever hear you laugh at him again!"

Still, a more complex and ultimately more positive kind of mediation is also available when hate speech occurs. One vitally important phase of a cultural-wealth curriculum consists in transforming an occasion on which a cultural liability such as racism or misogyny has been transmitted into an opportunity for passing down a cultural asset such as racial tolerance, a philosophy of antiracism, or the ideals of race and gender equality (cf. Carnes, 1999).

In that New England prep school, the original hate speech act and its target were announced at a school assembly and deplored by school officials. A school that mediates between children and the culture's stories will act differently. When a young boy calls a girl "dog" or "slut," when "Death Nigger" is scribbled on an African American child's locker, when "Gas for the Jew" is posted in the shower, teachers will respond to the injury done. They will also raise to consciousness the misogyny or the racism that the hate speech expresses, turn these into bona fide objects of study, and oversee student bookkeeping projects. In other words, an educational agent bent on the protection of children will proceed on the principle that one good way to vitiate a hidden curriculum is to move it into the curriculum proper. Then children and adults together can study the effects of hate speech on its targets, identify the attitudes that inform misogynous and racist speech, analyze the injuries it causes, explore the larger network of social practices in which this speech is embedded, track its modes of transmission, trace the history of both race and gender discrimination, and inquire into their moral and political significance.

CULTURAL CITIZENSHIP;
OR, WHOSE STOCK IS IT ANYWAY?

Some years ago, a PBS documentary showed an African American high school student damning the racial integration that his recent foremothers and -fathers had worked so hard to achieve. To the ears of one whose early schooling had taught her to believe that assimilation is the assured path to racial equality, he sounded sadly misguided, not to say ungrateful and ahistorical. When, however, I thought about the distinction between assimilation and acculturation and also reflected on Rousseau's distinction between active and passive citizenship, I began to sympathize with his charge.

As anthropologist Ralph Beals explains, assimilation is a one-way process. When acculturation occurs *both* parties to the transaction are affected, but in a clear case of assimilation an individual or a group replaces its original culture with a new one (Beals, 1953). Insisting that just about all members of U.S. society submit to the sovereign culture at school and in the public world, and keeping that culture intact by excluding men of non-European descent and virtually all women from actively contributing to it, we have tried to achieve assimilation pure and simple. Whether one considers this historical project to have been a success or a failure, by the time that television program was aired the price of assimilation had become an increasing fragmentation of American society along private cultural fault lines.

The kind of racial integration that many Americans, both Black and White, fought for in the past entailed bringing African Americans into the sovereign culture. It did not take into account the sovereign culture's willingness or unwillingness to allow them to bring with them some of their own cultural wealth. Had we as a nation opted for acculturation rather than assimilation, that high school student and his classmates might not have been so disaffected. Had we extended Rousseau's analysis of citizenship to the cultural arena, things might be different.

In *The Social Contract* Rousseau (1762/1947) distinguished between a person's being a passive and an active member of a state—in other words, between being subject to the law and being a participant in the sovereign authority, that is, a lawmaker. In what relation does the citizen of a democracy stand to the law? Rousseau's answer was that citizenship has a passive and an active side. In its passive form, a citizen's relationship to the law is that of sheer obedience. However, within a system of genuine self-government, which is what a democracy is supposed to be, a citizen is also active in that he is an author of the laws he obeys.

I say "he" advisedly. Rousseau introduced this active/passive distinction in order to show that a citizen of a democracy has a dual relationship to the state. That he then proceeded to restrict full citizenship to men and allow women only to be passive subjects of the law represents the fatal flaw in his final achievement. But despite this fundamental error, the contrast Rousseau drew between democracy and monarchy is instructive. Accept one or another nondemocratic form of government, and you are on shaky ground if you then complain that some group of people has been denied active citizenship. Cherish democracy and the injustice of excluding people from full participation in the state on the basis of their sex or race or ethnicity is evident.

As I thought about that disaffected high school student, it dawned on me that Rousseau's active/passive distinction applies to cultures as well as states. Or rather, it does once we broaden Rousseau's characterization of active citizenship.

Given the old narrow, reductive definition of culture as the higher learning, a concept of active cultural citizenship rooted in authorship is plausible. But with a more democratic definition of culture, the presumption that each item of wealth has an author or initial creator is not warranted. To be sure, there are many occasions on which it makes sense to presuppose a "prime mover" or "original creator." Most literary, artistic, scientific, and philosophical works are deliberate constructions—the products of individual people's creative labors. Granted, it is not always easy to determine whether, for example, Rodin was the "true" creator of the sculpture attributed to him or whether F. Scott Fitzgerald should be give sole credit for novels that relied so heavily on his wife's letters and journals. Granted, it can be highly misleading—sometimes downright unjust—to attribute a scientific discovery to just one or two individuals. Granted, even in cases in which authorship is undisputed, writers, painters, composers, sculptors, and scholars are aided and abetted by readers, listeners, reviewers, editors, publishers, and the like. Still, although the question of authorship may be far more complicated than is generally realized and is perhaps not even decidable in some cases, the assumption of a deliberate creator is plausible when items of cultural stock such as these are the issue.

An assumption of authorship makes no sense at all, however, when the cultural stock is the sort of thing that simply "emerged" or "grew" or "evolved." In *Guns, Germs, and Steel*, Jared Diamond went out of his way to dispel misconceptions about the origins of food production:

> What actually happened was not a *discovery* of food production, nor an *invention*, as we might first assume. There was often not even a conscious choice between food production and hunting-gathering . . . food production evolved as a by-product of decisions made without awareness of their consequences. (1999, pp. 105–106)

This holds true for huge portions of our culture's stock. With the help of Julia Morgan, William Randolph Hearst created—authored, if you will—his castle. But neither Dr. Benjamin Spock nor the writers of earlier baby manuals were the inventors of the child-care practices they codified. Dictionary makers do not invent languages, they codify them. The art of cooking predates the recipes of Fanny Farmer. Presumably, the sandwich was the invention of a British earl, but it is no use asking who invented bread, let alone who made the handshake, produced the Navajo language, or created a given group's or culture's healing techniques, housing forms, hunting practices, agricultural methods, religious rites, peacemaking activities, clothing regulations, children's games, or sexual mores.

Since these and most other items of cultural stock were not deliberately designed, authorship—however fuzzy this concept may be at its margins—is best regarded as but one form of active cultural citizenship. Is there another form?

Define active cultural citizenship in terms of the general category of making a contribution to the sovereign culture rather than the more specific one of authoring it. Now reflect on the fact that different groups in society have custody of different portions of stock. Add to this brew the question that cultural-reproduction theorists, feminist scholars, multiculturalists, and other skeptics are apt to ask when the subject is curriculum—namely, "Whose knowledge is it?" A very different form of active cultural citizenship then comes to light. Granted, the "whose knowledge" query is sometimes concerned solely with authorship. Far more often, however, those who ask it want to know the "social location" of the science or history or literature being transmitted to the next generation. From a cultural-wealth perspective, this translates into a query about which classes, which races, which genders have heretofore been the guardians of the stock at issue.

As anyone acquainted with George Bernard Shaw's play *Pygmalion* or its offspring *My Fair Lady* knows, patterns of speech, types of work, values such as neatness and cleanliness "belong," as it were, to different social classes. In the last decades of the 20th century an association between traits such as detachment and White, middle-class European men was also demonstrated, and scholars now believe that walking, talking, and even thinking are tied to gender, race, and class. I need hardly say that these linkages are neither hard and fast nor universal. On the contrary, they vary from one culture to another, and within a given culture they change over time, are modified by training, and are statistical in nature. Nonetheless, from the standpoint of a concept of cultural citizenship, it is important to know the social location of the stock that is included in a society's sovereign culture. Indeed, I would say that a societal group can be considered an active contributor to that culture just insofar as some reasonable portion of the stock in the group's custody is part of what the culture itself transmits to the next generation.

Now in Rousseau's philosophy every citizen of a democracy is an author of the laws that he obeys. In light of how little cultural stock is actually authored, it would make a mockery of the concept of active cultural citizenship to require that every citizen be a cultural author. Granted, each one of us is a transmitter of cultural stock, but this in itself does not make each one of us that stock's creator or originator. However, when a group is an acknowledged contributor to the culture's heritage, by proxy every member of the group can be thought of as partaking of active cultural citizenship.

To take the idea of active cultural citizenship one step further, I would say that in a cultural democracy, every guardian of cultural stock is by definition entitled to be an active contributor to the culture of the society as a whole. By extension, then, every individual has a right to active cultural citizenship. Of course, in the name of autonomy or separatism or on some other ground altogether, a group might refuse to contribute to the general stockpile. In such a case its members would still *have* a right to be active cultural citizens; they would simply not be *exercising* that right.

The arbitrary exclusion of certain social groups from the category of cultural contributor is perhaps at present a more realistic scenario in the United States than this "separatist" one, however. As a case in point, those African American high school students in the documentary were being treated by both school and society solely as passive members of U.S. culture. They were expected to live under its sway, yet by virtue of their group membership they were barred from being active contributors to the sovereign culture.

In some countries any person whose parents were themselves born there is both an active and a passive subject of the state, whereas an individual born of immigrant parents is allowed to be only the latter. As such nations deny active *political* citizenship to people of foreign origin, the United States has been loath to grant active *cultural* citizenship to men of non-European origin and to any but a few token women. Compelling all children to study the Western heritage and expecting them in adulthood to transmit this body of wealth to their offspring, our schools, colleges, and universities have told a large portion of the citizenry to rest content with being Western culture's passive subjects. It has been assumed that men of European descent—most particularly those from northern Europe—have the right to contribute to the sovereign culture even as they conform to its strictures. All others have been expected to internalize its norms, embrace its ideals, and adopt its ways of seeing, thinking, and behaving, with little hope of ever playing a more active role.

The point I wish to make is a variant of Rousseau's: In a democracy with a diverse population—a "culturally pluralist democracy," if you will—each individual ought to stand in a dual relationship to both the sovereign law and the sovereign culture. Perhaps in a culturally homogeneous democracy the ideals of justice and fairness would not require the extension of the full rights of cultural citizenship to the few citizens who diverged from the norm. In a country such as the United States whose population has from the beginning been marked by gender, ethnic, racial, and religious diversity, however, it is as unjust to limit active cultural citizenship to a chosen few as it is to restrict active political citizenship. At a time when the composition of the U.S. population has radically shifted and there is greater diversity than ever, it is also a dangerous policy.

One argument that is frequently offered in defense of restricting active cultural citizenship is that the sovereign culture of the United States has until recently been a unified whole and that a unitary culture is a prerequisite for a unified people. Suppose that the premise is true: Suppose U.S. culture has been unitary. It simply does not follow that a culture that is a unified whole necessarily possesses unifying or centripetal force. Indeed, when the price a society pays for cultural unity is the restriction of active cultural citizenship to a privileged few, alienation of at least some members of the excluded groups is to be expected. As that television documentary made all too clear, instead of resting content with being passive subjects of but not active contributors to the sovereign culture, all too many of the "culturally disenfranchised" are in fact becoming active resisters.

There is a dreadful irony here. Believing that when people hold on too firmly to their family or "private" cultural identities their divided loyalties may cause a culture to fall apart, many in the United States want everyone to assimilate to the old sovereign culture. But perceiving universal active cultural citizenship to be a threat to the unity of U.S. culture, they deny the majority of the population the right to contribute to it, thus driving them back in anger into their private cultural worlds.

There is no doubt about it. Rejecting Western culture on the grounds that it is a White male construct, the students I saw on television were angrily retreating into a kind of despair verging on group solipsism. Insisting that race or ethnicity is the only difference that makes a difference and espousing a norm of nonassociation with others, they were displaying hostility to the idea of finding the very commonalties among people that might serve the cause of unity. To be sure, the film may have exaggerated the extent of the fragmentation. But unless what was shown was actually manufactured, our concern is warranted.

Imagine now a school that has a cultural-wealth curriculum in place. Here the disaffected students can conduct cultural-wealth research projects that ask "Whose stock is it anyway?" Students can check the shelves of the school library and review course syllabi to determine which portions of cultural wealth authored by or otherwise relating to African Americans this educational agent is actually transmitting. Focusing on their school's hidden curriculum, they can seek to discover whether cultural liabilities regarding race are being passed down and, if so, by what mechanisms. They can also track the life and times of their own alienation from both school and society. And, in the manner of those Syracuse University researchers, they can identify and track the activities of nonschool guardians of stock such as local bookstores, newspapers, community associations, and even Web sites.

Granted, these projects might uncover evidence that angers African American and other minority students—for example, of the denigration of their art and literature or the devaluation of their group's history. Yet fact-finding can lead to change. Suppose the students present their data at a school forum, as those Syracuse students did at a daylong town meeting. Suppose they invite representatives of other educational agents in their community to participate. Suppose they publish their findings on the cultural-wealth research Web site where they had posted their data as it was collected. Suppose they invite the entire student body to join in their research projects and use the results to do some cultural bookkeeping.

Responding to Hate At School has this to say about hate speech and hateful acts: "In secondary schools, no factor is more important to success than student involvement in suggesting and implementing solutions" (Carnes, 1999, p. 27). When student anger is harnessed to constructive purposes, it can transmute into effective action. And what is more constructive than contributing to the solution of the problem of cultural miseducation—on the one hand by raising the consciousness of the school community about the importance of cultural bookkeeping and of the research it requires; and, on the other, by the cultural-wealth data the young bookkeepers produce? Who knows. If these efforts create a groundswell of cultural-wealth researchers and bookkeepers, they might even bring closer the day when a universal right to active cultural citizenship becomes a reality.

Needless to say, in recommending that so-called marginalized groups and their members be granted full cultural citizenship, I am not suggesting that every item belonging to the culture of every such group should be incorporated into the sovereign culture of the United States. On the contrary, every culture is necessarily selective.

The extension of passive but not active cultural citizenship to all is a redescription of Beals's assimilation. Of course our culture's boundaries are not impermeable. Pizza, salsa, humus: In my lifetime some items of stock belonging to groups who have not been considered bona fide cultural contributors have gradually been incorporated into the larger culture. But the absorption of one or a few items that are located on the preservation continuum of an excluded group represents a kind of tokenism. It does not turn the group into a bona fide contributor to the sovereign wealth.

In contrast, the extension of active cultural citizenship to all approximates Beals's acculturation. A wonderful example of this process was reported by Nora Ellen Groce in *Everyone Here Spoke Sign Language* (1985; cf. Martin, 1992). The record shows that for 200 years, Martha's Vineyard, an island off the coast of Massachusetts, had an unusually high incidence of hereditary deafness. Amazingly, the island's deaf inhabitants were fully integrated into Vineyard society: They were active in town government and the local militia, they owned stores, and at least one was a minister. How is this possible? In the "up-island" section of Martha's Vineyard the hearing people were bilingual. Instead of deaf citizens having to learn to negotiate the spoken language of the majority, or else resort to the written word, sign language was part of the hearing majority's curriculum. As a result, deaf people were not considered handicapped; indeed, they were not even thought of as belonging to a group called "the deaf."

I take the Martha's Vineyard story to be a parable for our time, its lessons pertaining to curriculum and culture, school and society. Martha's Vineyard was clearly enriched by everyone's knowing sign language. The deaf inhabitants obviously gained, but so did the general up-island community: instead of having an "outcast" population draining its resources, the community found that its pool of talent was significantly increased. In addition, the hearing had at their command an alternate mode of communication.

In citing the case of Martha's Vineyard, I do not for a moment mean to take a stand on whether English should be the national language of the United States. A call for genuine acculturation rather than simple assimilation does not answer the question of *which* items now in the custody of a given race, class, gender, or ethnicity should be integrated into the larger common culture or even *from which* guardians the items should be drawn. Furthermore, to extend active cultural citizenship to all is no guarantee that the words or deeds of any given group will be incorporated into the sovereign culture. As the right to political citizenship entitles people to participate actively in the state but does not entail anyone's actual active participation, let alone that an individual's wishes will prevail, the right to full cultural citizenship simply entitles groups and by extension individuals to make significant contributions to the culture.

To some, the idea of a universal right to active cultural citizenship betokens anarchy and chaos. This false equation between cultural inclusiveness and disorder has a long history. In the *Republic*, Plato likened a democratic state to a ship whose sailors, knowing nothing of navigation, all want to steer. Executing their rivals and throwing them overboard, they drink and feast when they should be paying attention "to the seasons of the year, the sky, the stars, the winds" (1974, 488). Ever since, democracy's enemies have invoked the specter of chaos.

To be sure, the democratization of a society's common or sovereign culture—which is what a universal right to active cultural citizenship is all about—means that new "raw materials" will be on hand for the reconstruction of the concept of Western or European or U.S. culture. But while these may well introduce a greater degree of complexity into the process, the extension of active citizenship to all betokens neither political chaos nor an anarchic approach to values. I said earlier that rather than lapsing into a mindless value anarchism, a cultural-wealth perspective on education requires that distinctions be made between cultural assets and liabilities. A theory of democratic cultural citizenship also demands that these value distinctions be made.

Who is to draw these distinctions? Would that I could answer this here, but it is in fact one more of those big value questions that our culture—indeed every culture, whether democratized or not—must face. Like the others, it is not created by a cultural-wealth approach to education. A cultural-wealth perspective simply moves it out of the shadows and into the light.

CHAPTER 5

Maximizing the Assets

DISTRIBUTING THE HERITAGE;
OR, A TROUBLESOME DILEMMA

After graduation from college, I worked in the market research department of a large advertising agency. There I tallied responses to questionnaires about Johnny Mops, vacuum cleaners, and canned beef stew. One favorite memory of that period of my life is how drastically opinions varied on whether the beef stew contained too few or too many carrots. I must confess to wondering at the time if the evenly divided responses did not render our research pointless. When, four decades later, I encountered this same sort of discrepancy in the data I was collecting for research of my own, my attitude was not nearly so cavalier.

While attending a class reunion at the Little Red School House, I realized that my friends and I were the repositories of an important portion of our culture's wealth. And it occurred to me—no doubt because I was beginning to see education from a cultural vantage point—that as our generation died out, these assets would be lost to posterity. Becoming agitated at the thought, I approached the Spencer Foundation with the idea of preserving the memories of some of the "products" of progressive education.

The data that anthropologist Helena Ragoné and I collected more than vindicated my belief that when one takes the children's perspective, progressive education is seen in a new light. But I cite our project in these pages for another reason entirely. In answer to the question "What, if any, effect did attending a progressive school have on you?" a 60-year-old woman said that she remembers studying grammar and that it was very helpful later on when she studied languages in high school. In contrast, a 60-year-old man said that the great drawback of his early education was that he didn't learn a lot of things. For example, he was never taught grammar.

Does it really matter that individuals who were in the very same classrooms from ages 5 to 13 have such wildly divergent memories of their schooling? I would say it does. For if the memories are true, our culture's ability to realize its cherished ideals of equality and self-government is called into question. Many people take it for granted that to achieve a fair and equitable distribution of the culture's wealth, everyone's curriculum—not of course their vocational or professional curriculum, but the curriculum of what is usually called "general" education—must be the same. Sometimes special groups such as children with disabilities have been exempted from this dictum. Yet those who advocate equal treatment for such groups have tended to insist that their general education should be the same as everyone else's.

Certainly, on the day I presented a paper on the "There's Too Much to Teach" problem to the annual meeting of the Great Britain Philosophy of Education Society, this assumption was operative. When I finished my presentation, several members of the audience told me in no uncertain terms that an equitable solution to the problem of superabundance could not be found. The culture reproduces itself through the mechanisms of a school curriculum and tracking system that distribute different portions of the culture's capital to children from different social classes, they said. Given the class systems of both Britain and the United States, how can anyone possibly think that a fair distribution of cultural capital is to be had?

To this point I have barely discussed the distribution of a culture's wealth. Yet the questions "Who are the recipients of the stock being passed down to the next generation?," "Is the legacy being divided equally?," "Should identical portions of the heritage be transmitted to all or should different people receive different portions?" are every bit as important to ask as "Does the stock constitute an asset or a liability?" And from the standpoint of the "cultural-reproduction theorists"—a.k.a. "critical capital theorists"—at that Sunday morning session at Oxford's New College, questions regarding distribution are the main thing.

Cultural-reproduction theorists are an exception to my rule that in this day and age we tend to look at education only from the standpoint of the individual. Briefly put, they argue that schools are not the neutral, objective observers of the cultural, economic, and political scene most people think they are. On the contrary, in stratified societies such as our own, schools distribute "cultural capital" unevenly, thus reproducing the existing class structure. More particularly, these theorists maintain that through intricate tracking systems and other mechanisms, schools pass down the cultural capital of the dominant class to the children of that class while denying the children of other classes access to that capital (see, e.g., Apple, 1979; Giroux, 1981).

Different thinkers offer different formulations of this "reproduction thesis." But the details of the disputes about its degree of determinism, its portrayal of students as passive subjects, and its application to gender need not detain us. Furthermore, reproduction theory's contribution to the study of education actually extends well beyond the reproduction thesis. There is, in the first place, the central insight that the distribution pattern of schooling is highly politicized. To this must be added the claim that decisions about what gets included in school's curriculum are themselves politicized. And there is also the devastating critique that in abstracting school from its cultural and political contexts, educational researchers create the illusion of both their own and school's objectivity.

What matters when the subject is cultural miseducation, however, is that reproduction theorists have focused on just one portion of the culture's stock—what they refer to as cultural capital. I leave open here the question of the relationship between cultural capital and what Robert Putnam and others call "social capital." For my point is simply that although the category of cultural capital includes far more than propositional knowledge, it is not nearly as inclusive as the idea of cultural stock outlined here. In addition, although one of the founding fathers of reproduction theory, French sociologist Pierre Bourdieu, has conducted important studies of nonschool agents, the theory's adherents have been mainly concerned with just one educational agent, and that is school.

Finally, reproduction theorists have for the most part concentrated on just one dimension of the cultural-wealth perspective that I have been formulating here—the distribution of a culture's stock. Insofar as transmission mechanisms such as tracking appear to be implicated in the uneven distribution of stock that they discern, they also attend to these, but this interest derives from a primary concern with distribution. The intense interest in the "Whose knowledge is it?" question also stems from a concern with distribution. After all, to demonstrate that school passes down knowledge according to class lines—or, as some would insist, class and gender lines—it must be shown that the knowledge at issue is already class property.

In sum, the reproductionist approach to education differs in both scope and intent from the cultural-wealth approach I offer in these pages. The latter is guided by a desire to solve the problem of generations and thereby reduce, if not actually eliminate, cultural miseducation. To accomplish this it is necessary to know the extent and nature of our culture's stock and its educational agents, and to discover whether and how our assets and liabilities are being preserved and transmitted to the new generation. With this in mind, I have developed a systematic conceptual framework that allows for the tracking of cultural assets and liabilities across the whole society. The object of reproduction theory is very different, and its scope is not nearly so broad.

The cultural-reproduction theorists at that Oxford meeting are by no means the only ones to import economic language into educational discourse (see, e.g., Oakeshott, 1967). Nor are they alone in assuming that the sole remedy for an unjust class-based distribution of the wealth is to mandate the same curriculum for all. Yet the policy of "the same legacy for all" greatly exacerbates the problem created by the superabundance of wealth. Indeed, it makes it enormously difficult, if not impossible, to maximize the assets a culture passes down to its young.

Just what is to count as "the same" or "roughly the same" curriculum is once again a pragmatic matter. For some purposes and in some contexts, the fact that the junior high curriculum of one of my sons included cooking, sewing, wood shop, and metal shop along with the usual academic subjects, whereas the other son's did not, would be sufficient reason to say that the two boys studied different curricula. In other contexts or for other purposes, the differences in question might not be thought to make a difference. Be this as it may, the assumption that the curriculum of general education should be roughly the same for everyone—this translates into the expectation that everyone will acquire the same portion of our heritage—turns the fact of abundance into an intractable problem.

Nonetheless, educational theorists of all stripes insist that universal suffrage and universal schooling—where this latter is equated with the same general course of study for all, although not necessarily the same methods of instruction—"are inextricably bound together" (Adler, 1982, p. 3). From a cultural-wealth perspective, the presumption seems to be that those who study the same curriculum will inherit the same parcels of stock. And it is taken as gospel that democratic self-government requires identical holdings on the part of all.

In light of the thesis that both political democracy and social equality mandate the policy of one curriculum for all, the discrepant memories about grammar of our interviewees take on special significance. On the one hand, they compel us to ask: Are the ideals of democracy and social equality unattainable if different portions of the culture's stock are passed down to different portions of the population? On the other hand, they make one wonder whether we face a troubling dilemma: Either give up hope of maximizing the transmission of cultural wealth to the next generation or forsake the basic political and social commitments of democracy. For it is patently impossible to transmit *all* of a culture's wealth to any given person, let alone to *every* person. There is so much cultural stock to pass down that the pressing practical problem is not the usual one of stretching resources so that everyone will get an adequate share. Rather it is that of selecting from our resources so that they will be adequately represented.

IDENTICAL INHERITANCES; OR, THE ARGUMENT FROM DEMOCRATIC CITIZENSHIP

"Your son should learn to play the piano before he takes up the trumpet," an acquaintance once told me. When I replied that he had studied the recorder for a year and had become adept at reading music, and that he had meanwhile fallen in love with the sound of trumpets, she reaffirmed that every music student must first learn the piano. When I voiced my opinion that there was more than one route to becoming a trumpet player, she threw up her hands in despair.

The assumption that there is one right curriculum for all budding musicians is a special case of the more general thesis that whatever educational end is put forward, there is one right way to achieve it. The supposition that every citizen of a democracy must study the same curriculum—or, in cultural-wealth terms, that identical portions of stock must be transmitted to all—is another instance of this rule.

In view of the superabundance of stock and the enormous range of nonschool educational agents, it is of course extremely implausible to suppose that *identical* portions of stock could ever be transmitted to *all* members of the next generation. When education is equated with schooling, the goal of identical inheritances may seem at first glance to make sense. But once the very different kinds of homes, families, religious organizations, and peer groups—in fact, different everythings—contained in contemporary democratic societies are acknowledged, the absurdity of assuming that a general education will transmit identical legacies to all is evident.

In addition, the conflicting memories about grammar of my two classmates strongly suggest that even when education and schooling are equated, the prospects of passing down identical fortunes to all children are dim. True, one or the other of our informants may have been subject to false memories. Or, just as another classmate was in his own words "out to lunch" during his elementary school years, our male interviewee may have been out to lunch on what, according to my memory, were the relatively few occasions on which our school taught us grammar. Still, the fact remains that there is no guarantee that those who are taught the same material will end up having learned the same material, let alone in the same way, shape, or form. Indeed, given everything we know about individual and group differences, there is ample reason to suppose the opposite.

Absurd or not, reality or fantasy, the idea that the same educational goal mandates the same curriculum has a long history. Braving the ridicule of his colleagues, in Book V of Plato's *Republic* Socrates argued that the men and women who were destined to rule the Just State of his imagination should receive identical training. Now Plato was no democrat; hence he did not prescribe the same education for everyone. But his unexamined assumption that those destined for the same role in society should pursue the same curriculum is the very one that citizens of the United States and other 21st century democracies adhere to. Of course it is recognized that individual differences are sometimes best met by different methods of instruction. In the face of differences in abilities, some educational thinkers say that certain students should only be required to learn the rudiments of one or another subject whereas others should go on to master said subject in depth. And even some of the fiercest advocates of the same education for all allow choice in the area of foreign-language study. With such minor qualifications, however, and with the added assumption that every nation will stress the study of its own history, the policy of identical inheritances is taken for granted.

At first glance Plato's postulate of same role, same curriculum seems incontrovertible. Surely, those who must eventually perform the same tasks and shoulder the same responsibilities will have to study the same subjects, will require the same training. Yet there are at least two circumstances in which the same societal role does not demand the same education.

Suppose a given role can be performed in different ways. Take as an example the role of school principal. Suppose that one way of carrying out the principal role involves looking "inward"; for instance, befriending the teaching staff, knowing all the children's names, being accessible to parents, and generally making one's primary goal the improvement of the quality of life in school. And suppose that another way of being a principal involves looking "outward"; for instance, representing the school's interests to members of the central administration, speaking publicly on pressing educational issues, and generally making one's primary goal the enhancement of the school's reputation in the community. Insofar as different ways of performing a given role involve the expression of different attitudes, the exercise of different skills, and the application of different knowledge, it stands to reason that different courses of study could constitute preparation for the selfsame role.

Furthermore, so long as dependence on others for knowledge, skill, and the like is permitted, this postulate of same role, same curriculum need not be accepted. For if someone else can perform one of the duties your role requires of you—for instance, drawing up a school budget or writing speeches—or if someone else can supply you with the requisite knowledge that you lack, quite different curricula could be designed for those who would perform the same role.

The question is: Are these two exceptions operative when the role at issue is citizenship in a democracy? Even supposing that the citizen role can be performed in alternative ways, is there not a core of knowledge, skill, attitudes, and values that everyone must acquire? Because a citizen in a democracy is supposed to be a decision maker, many educational thinkers have assumed so (e.g., Adler, 1982; Meier, 1995; Scheffler, 1973; White, 1983; Wolff, 1970). Nevertheless, if citizens of a democracy could lean on one another for their knowledge, skills, attitudes, and perhaps even values, the assumption that there is an essential core to be mastered would not support the conclusion of the same curriculum for all. Suppose, for example, that I study mathematics and psychology and you learn science and sociology and we pool our knowledge. Working together we could jointly make decisions utilizing all four subjects.[1]

Yet is a cooperative model of decision making sufficiently democratic? Doesn't democracy require every citizen to be a self-governing, autonomous individual and doesn't this preclude our leaning on one another for knowledge and the rest?

As Plato long ago demonstrated, self-government does not entail absolute self-sufficiency. Although his rulers were to be self-legislating, they would also be dependent. "Not one of us is self-sufficient, but needs many things," said Plato's Socrates as he and his companions thought away existing institutions and in their imaginations witnessed the birth of a city (1974, 369b). "As they need many things, people make use of one another for various purposes," Socrates continued (369c). For the record, Rousseau's fictional boy Émile—often taken by philosophers to be the very model of an autonomous or self-governing person and intended by Rousseau to become a full-fledged citizen of a democracy—is also deeply dependent on others, most notably his wife Sophie (Martin, 1985).

Still, although Plato and Rousseau built dependency on others for their creature comforts into the lives of their respective citizen-rulers, both men expected the latter to be intellectually self-reliant individuals. Supposing the self-government required by the citizens of a democracy does not entail *absolute* self-reliance, isn't absolute *intellectual* self-reliance still required? Rousseau believed it is, and many contemporary educational theorists seem to agree with him.

"Every citizen should speak his opinion entirely from himself," Rousseau wrote in *The Social Contract* (1762/1947, p. 27), adding, "Each

---

[1]Whether the three Rs represent an exception to the findings of this chapter I leave an open question.

citizen should be perfectly independent of each of his fellow citizens" (p. 49). Two centuries later echoes of this sentiment could still be heard. Thus one late-20th-century thinker wrote, "The contemporary American citizen has an obligation to master enough modern science to enable him to follow debates about nuclear policy and come to an independent conclusion" (Wolff, 1970, p. 17). Another analyst of education said that since every responsible citizen "will have to arrive at her own assessment," she must "enjoy a broad curriculum including, for instance, mathematics, the human and physical sciences, history and the arts" (White, 1983, p. 83). And in the name of citizenship, a third commentator wanted to require everyone to master language, literature, the fine arts, mathematics, natural science, history, geography, and social studies (Adler, 1982).

In an age of superabundance—especially the overabundance of highly technical knowledge—this vision of unencumbered citizens making definitive judgments about the common good without any help from others embodies an impossible ideal of citizenship, democratic or otherwise. Just imagine everyone knowing enough about science and nuclear policy, economics and fiscal policy, psychology and mental health policy, biology and genetic engineering policy, chemistry and drug policy, and so forth to make their own "perfectly independent" decisions!

Now consider the case of Ken Harrison, the protagonist of a play that tests to its very limits Plato's insight that human dependency and individual self-governance can go hand in hand (Clark, 1978). In *Whose Life Is It Anyway?*, Harrison, paralyzed from the neck down, is completely dependent on others for the performance of what are to able-bodied individuals the simplest tasks. In addition, as a sculptor untrained in law and medicine, he must rely on others and on books that others read to him for the information and for the legal and medical expertise he needs to make and carry out decisions of his own. Despite his almost total lack of self-reliance, he proves himself as capable of self-governance as anyone, even in regard to that most fateful decision of whether to continue living. Whether or not one agrees with his choice to take his own life, whether or not one sympathizes with the doctor who tries to prevent him in that one instance from being a self-determining agent, one cannot doubt Harrison's capacity to make responsible decisions.

If Ken Harrison can rely on others for knowledge and skill yet be his own legislator, so can the rest of us. But suppose one agrees that intellectual self-governance does not require absolute self-reliance. Doesn't the latter constitute an ideal to be pursued? Not in my opinion.

I cite the case of Ken Harrison to demonstrate that decision making *can* be rational and responsible even if the agent relies on others for the knowledge involved in it. In fact, however, self-governance inevitably involves elements of dependency. After all, someone who has managed to master the knowledge relevant to public policy matters will have relied on teachers, textbook writers, and other experts in the course of attaining that standard. Besides, those who did the research that provided the basis for the teaching and the texts were themselves dependent on others.

As a case in point, consider that fateful moment in the search for the structure of DNA when Jerry Donahue, an American scientist, told James Watson that the scheme the latter believed would solve the problem could not work. Since its publication in 1968, Watson's *The Double Helix* has been read as a story of competition in science. However, even as it reported a race to the Nobel Prize, it depicted dependence and interdependence at the farthest reaches of knowledge. The book's protagonist is not a lone, self-reliant scientist but a "couple," Watson and Francis Crick, who leaned on one another for knowledge and skill as well as for ideas and inspiration. They were of necessity dependent on others, too. Except for Linus Pauling, "Jerry Donahue knew more about hydrogen bonds than anyone else in the world," wrote Watson (1968, p. 122), who protested vigorously to Donahue that his—Watson's—own scheme faithfully followed the appropriate pictures in the organic-chemistry texts. As Watson told the story, when a day later he, Watson, came up with a different scheme, a double helix, before Crick ever arrived on the scene he asked if Donahue had any objections to it. Donahue had none.

Donahue is not the only person on whom Watson and Crick relied. Rosalind Franklin's experimental data played an essential role in their discovery (Sayre, 1975; Watson, 1968). In addition, their work was informed by Crick's earlier collaboration with Bill Cochran, Pauling's classic book *The Nature of the Chemical Bond*, the papers of J. M. Gilland and D. O. Jordan, a classic paper by J. D. Bernal and I. Fankuchen, the theoretical chemist John Griffith's calculations, and a Cavendish Laboratory machinist's models (Watson, 1968). There is no reason to suppose that this list is exhaustive. Indeed, one of the most interesting, albeit seldom noted, aspects of the race described in *The Double Helix* is just how little Crick and Watson knew. Watson reported, for instance, that he could not understand large sections of that Bernal and Fankuchen paper. Crick, in turn, was forced to confess to one of the world's leading DNA experts that he did not remember certain chemical differences.

Defenders of the thesis that intellectual self-reliance is essential to democratic citizenship might of course say that the case of Watson and Crick is as unrepresentative as that of Ken Harrison. While agreeing that the two men functioned as an intellectually interdependent couple and were also dependent on others, they will insist that our concern is citizenship, not science. And supposing they admit that a paraplegic is capable of self-government, and that even the most creative scientists are not wholly self-reliant, they will say that so long as self-governance is essential to democratic citizenship, one curriculum is required of all.

But is self-government a requisite of citizenship in a democracy? The question is ambiguous. It goes without saying that the citizenry of a democracy must be self-governing. But it does not follow from this truism that *every* member of a self-governing citizenry has to be his or her own legislator. If a glee club sings beautifully, does it follow that every one of its members sings beautifully? Surely not. If an army is strong, does it follow that every man and woman in it is strong? To suppose so is to commit what logic teachers and textbooks call the fallacy of division. Granted, there might not be any sour notes in a beautifully singing glee club or weaklings in a strong army. But to know that an attribute of a collectivity such as a glee club or an army is "distributed out" to each member of the collectivity requires a thoroughgoing examination of the case at hand.

One of Rousseau's contributions to the theory of democracy was to "distribute out" self-governance—to make being one's own legislator an attribute of every member of a democratic citizenry, not just of the citizenry as a whole. Whether this philosophical move accomplished his goal of legitimating obedience to law has long been debated by political theorists and philosophers. Whether it is otherwise justified is another one of those complex and highly controversial issues that cannot possibly be decided here. Nor need it be. For suppose that those who say that every citizen of a democracy must be self-governing, albeit not absolutely self-sufficient, are correct. Even then there is no need for everyone to study the same curriculum.

Nor is the less stringent version of the demand for identical inheritances—namely, that everyone's general curriculum must at least have a common core—warranted. When *Cultural Literacy*—a book containing a 67-page appendix listing "What Literate Americans Need to Know"—was published (Hirsch, 1987), a new game sprang up. Instead of asking one another why anyone would think that Americans really need to know what "a capella" means, who Omar Bradley was, or where Hudson Bay is, members of the citizenry measured their own and their friends' erudition by this yardstick. No doubt some who played the game were mocking the items on the list. Some may even have been ridiculing the very idea of such a list. Yet game and book tapped into an impulse toward educational conformity that is so widespread among literate Americans and so strong as to qualify as a cultural compulsion.

Where citizenship is concerned nobody says, "Here's one way to educate citizens. Can anyone think of another?" Someone constructs a list of concepts for everyone to learn. Dissatisfied, someone else draws up a list of facts for each of us to commit to memory. Disdaining lists of unrelated items, a third person offers a list of intellectual disciplines for all to study. Saying there is no need for everyone to have the same knowledge, a fourth submits a list of skills for Mr. Everyman and Ms. Everywoman to acquire.

How subjective the various lists are! I at least can think of no objective reason why *every* citizen of the United States has to have a firm grasp of physics, or perhaps of psychology or the history of art; why *everyone* must know in what war the Battle of the Bulge occurred or to what text "No man is an island" belongs. I certainly agree that these items of cultural wealth should be passed down to *some* members of the citizenry as living legacy. But in view of the overabundance of our culture's wealth, it makes far more sense to me to figure out how to transmit as many of our assets as we can and how to distribute them as fairly as possible rather than devote our energies to distributing the same tiny portion of our accumulated stock to everyone.

I am also astonished by how ready people are to generate new lists when the old ones are challenged and how quickly the requirements can pile up. One or more sciences are on your list? If there is one right curriculum for becoming a self-governing citizen, is there not also one right curriculum—albeit a different one—for acquiring competence in these fields? And if that one right curriculum involves attaining competence in mathematics, as it probably does, must not a citizen first pursue that other course of study?

Is critical thinking the primary item on your list of what every citizen of a democracy must learn? To think critically a person has to be able to spot logical fallacies, identify arguments, isolate assumptions, and assess conclusions. If there is one right curriculum for becoming a citizen, why not also one right curriculum for each constituent skill of critical thinking?

The compulsory universal curriculum route fast becomes a veritable obstacle course. Some may protest that the one right curriculum policy applies only to citizenship in a democracy. But if the policy does not hold true for other goals, why suppose that it applies to citizenship? Why start down the compulsory curriculum path in the first place?

DIFFERENT LEGACIES;
OR, THE ARGUMENT FROM SOCIAL EQUALITY

When I first began writing about the ideas I have just presented, I had an unforgettable encounter with a book editor. Unaware that, over lunch, the female half of his publishing team had expressed interest in my book proposal, this man had only to hear that in my prospective book I planned to challenge the idea of the same curriculum for all to spring to his feet. "We do not publish racist works," he shouted as he ushered me out the door.

There is nothing racist about calling the belief in transmitting exactly the same portfolio of stock to all an impossible dream. Still, to do the man justice, there is no doubt that both historically and philosophically speaking, different curricula have all too often been designed with different and unequal societal roles in mind.

The corollary of Plato's same role, same curriculum assumption is the postulate that those destined to play different societal roles should receive different educations. In the Just State of the *Republic* where there are three different societal roles—those of ruler, warrior, and artisan—this translates into a separate curriculum track for each. Now it is not entirely clear if Plato considered these roles to be unequal. By 21st-century standards, however, they are precisely that, if for no other reason than that those who do not rule Plato's Just State are obliged to obey those who do.

In striking contrast to his hero's class-bound utopia, Rousseau envisioned a state in which all men would govern. A firm believer in the same role, same curriculum postulate, he therefore assumed that, ideally, every boy would receive the same items of cultural stock as every other. For Rousseau, the education of girls was a different matter. Whereas boys in his philosophy were destined to be active citizens of his democracy, girls would grow up to be good wives, mothers, and homemakers. Following Plato's lead that different roles demand different curricula, Rousseau therefore designed separate tracks for the two sexes. In an introduction to a 1979 edition of *Émile*, the translator wrote that what Rousseau attempts "is to present an egalitarian politics that rivals Plato's politics in moral appeal" (1762/1979, p. 6). Read carefully what Rousseau had to say about the education of the girl Sophie, and especially about her having to learn to obey even Émile's unjust commands, however, and the claim that *Émile* contains an egalitarian politics evaporates.

One need look no further than Mary Wollstonecraft's *A Vindication of the Rights of Woman*, published in England just 30 years after *Émile*, to know that the two-track gender-based curriculum system Rousseau proposed for males and females had historical as well as philosophical roots. One has only to read about the 19th century's vocational education movement in the United States to know that the different educations Plato proposed for his rulers and his artisans has also had real-life counterparts. But the fact that a policy of different curricula is likely to be racist—or sexist or classist or all three—if it is tied to unequal societal roles does not mean that the policy itself is wedded to inequality. It does not mean that different curricula cannot prepare people for the same role. It does not mean that equality always and everywhere requires the same curriculum for all.

In company with so many others, that irate publisher treated the same role, same curriculum postulate as an article of faith. If I had stayed to argue my case, he undoubtedly would have insisted that a single school curriculum for all is too precious an ideal to challenge. There are, however, three good reasons for rejecting the policy.

The first and most obvious argument against a one-curriculum-for-all policy is that it introduces a strong dose of compulsion into education. Although the range of subjects held to be essential to individual decision making may seem enormous when mastery is the issue, it is quite narrow when judged in relation to student interests and abilities. Those blessed with artistic gifts, mechanical aptitude, or what has been called "bodily-kinesthetic intelligence" (Gardner, 1983) may well find it impossible to relate to any courses in their curriculum. Those with, for instance, a decided scientific or literary bent will have to study subjects they cannot abide. It has rightly been said that "Compulsion is not coercion: the gentlest of methods is compatible with a compulsory system" (White, 1973, p. 89). Still, it is no accident that a compulsory curriculum normally carries in its wake an impressive coercive apparatus. When the opportunities for choice are diminished in education, boredom, inattention, and a lack of motivation create the need for external prods and sanctions.

Second, when the same school curriculum is prescribed for all, individual interests and abilities get short shrift and difference is perceived as deficiency. In defending the premise of the same course of study for all against the objection that it overlooks differences among people, one prominent educator first invoked the same role, same curriculum postulate: Since all children in the United States will grow up to be citizens, they must have the same education. Then he asked what can be done "to cope" with individual differences. Adjust the program so that children who "manifest deficiencies that would result in their not achieving the requisite standard of performance" are given "truly remedial" help, he said (Adler, 1982, p. 44). This slide from difference to deficiency, from an objection to a proposal based on the appreciation of variety to a reply that presupposes the need for remedy, is not surprising. When little room is reserved for individuality in an educational scheme, it is far easier to treat difference as a problem to be overcome than to acknowledge that one price of the plan is the reduction of the individuality that many have wanted education in a democratic society to encourage.

A third good reason for rejecting the policy of one curriculum for all is that its implicit endorsement of the goal of absolute self-sufficiency leads to the equation of dependence on others with personal inadequacy and failure. Instead of being taught the lesson that Watson and Crick had somehow learned by heart—namely, that the knowledge and skill you do not yourself possess can be had from others—students learn that if they do not meet the standard of performance set for them, they are not capable of participating in discussions of public policy. Instead of being taught how to get the knowledge and skill that they lack when they need it, they will come to believe that their intellectual reliance on others impairs their ability to make rational decisions.

In pointing out the impossibility of achieving absolute self-reliance and the undesirability of holding it up as an ideal to strive for, I do not mean to deny the importance of everyone's becoming self-reliant in some respects and to some degree. Of course, whenever it is possible, children should, in Maria Montessori words, "learn to walk without assistance, to run, to go up and down stairs, to lift up fallen objects, to dress and undress themselves, to bathe themselves, to speak distinctly, and to express their own needs clearly" (1912/1964, p. 97). But although, other things being equal, the goal of self-reliance encompasses many more actions than are on Montessori's list, it is unrealistic to demand that it include all actions and quite misleading to suggest that it is the essence of self-government. It is also counterproductive.

Denied the lesson that dependency on others is perfectly compatible with self-government, school's dropouts are all too apt to become democracy's delinquents. Even the best and brightest students are likely to suffer a paralysis because of their relative ignorance. Despite one philosopher's disclaimer that "policy very rarely turns on disputes over technical or theoretical details" (Wolff, 1970, p. 17), they, too, must depend on others for a good deal of the knowledge relevant to public policy decisions. When self-reliance is held up as the ideal, the evident need for an education that portrays dependency in a positive light is not even recognized.

Those who automatically equate the policy of different curricula for different people with racism do not think along these lines, however. They fear that a policy of curricular difference will inevitably give rise to inequalities. Wouldn't people who learned, say, physics, mathematics, and computer science have the greatest earning power and the highest social status? Wouldn't they—or else those who studied some other designated set of subjects, such as microbiology, computer science, and economics—end up making public policy decisions for the rest of us? A related risk is that curricular difference will encourage exploitation. Wouldn't those who pursued one course of study be in a position to acquire and use the knowledge and skill that others possess without paying back in kind?

Inequality and exploitation are very real dangers when a policy of different curricula for different people is accompanied by an ideal of absolute self-reliance. And I do not want to deny that, at present, U.S. culture is committed to this latter (cf. Bellah et al., 1985). But one who acknowledges the illusory nature of total self-reliance and is willing to substitute for it an ideal of social interdependence can pursue the strategy of different curricula—if not with impunity, at least in the knowledge that the evils I have listed are not its inevitable outcomes.

The question is: In view of the difficulties inherent in any project of social and political reconstruction, would it not be wise to beat a retreat from educational difference to the seemingly safer ground of curricular sameness? In my judgment it would not be. It is not just that in adopting sameness as educational policy one is apt to do more harm than good. Nor is it just that the policy turns the question of what should be taught—one that surely deserves to be treated contextually—into an abstract query that invites unrealistic responses. Given the superabundance of cultural wealth, when one curriculum is mandated for all, it becomes virtually impossible to solve the educational problem of generations. Even if we stanched the flow of cultural liabilities, we would not be in a position to maximize the transmission of cultural assets to our young. And this latter is of crucial importance if only because some of our culture's liabilities are all too likely to persist as living legacies when alternative ways of acting and living are forgotten.

I am the first to agree that adoption of a policy of different curricula for different people will not cause the problem of abundance to vanish. It will, however, alleviate it. In the ideal case, a policy of curricular difference would allow a culture's entire wealth to be represented in the curriculum of the whole society—although not the curriculum of each individual. In contrast, because the policy of same role, same curriculum requires the same portion of those assets be "mapped" onto every individual in society, significant loss of cultural wealth is all but guaranteed.

The educational theories of Plato and Rousseau illustrate my point. As I have said, both men took the postulate of different educations for different people as their starting points. Dividing the population into three groups or classes, Plato solved the problem of abundance—which was admittedly much less severe in his day than ours—by assigning a different body of knowledge, skill, and so on to each one. Rejecting Plato's substantive account of the different groups in society, Rousseau nevertheless approached the problem of abundance in Plato's way. Dividing the population of his ideal society into two sexes—men and women—he, too, assigned a different body of knowledge, skill, and so forth to each. Although these strategies may not have succeeded in transmitting to the next generation the entire body of cultural wealth, both Plato and Rousseau nevertheless achieved greater representation of that heritage than we do today.

It is a commonplace that from the standpoint of who should rule the state, Plato was an elitist. Denying full citizenship to women, Rousseau was one, too. However, from the standpoint of what constitutes cultural wealth and, consequently, should be included in a society's curriculum, Plato and Rousseau were better democrats than most contemporary educational thinkers. Granted, they drew distinctions of value within the cultural heritage; granted, each man wanted the individuals he designated as rulers to be taught the body of knowledge, skill, and so forth he deemed most important. Still, these political elitists included in the education of at least *some* individuals important parts of our cultural wealth whose existence is scarcely acknowledged today.

Think of Rousseau's two-track approach to the question of what should be taught. Committed to a gender-based division of tasks and responsibilities on the grounds that sex or gender is the only difference that makes a difference, he mapped one part of what he took to be his culture's wealth onto the curriculum of boys and another part onto that of girls. Despite his project's serious flaws, it did have one great strength. Rejecting the idea of designing a curriculum for anyone that transmitted the whole heritage but including in the curriculum of *some* people—namely, girls and women—the cultural wealth associated with the world of the private home and family, Rousseau succeeded better than we do in making the curriculum of the whole society approximate the whole inheritance. Having finally carried out Wollstonecraft's project of rejecting the education Rousseau designed for Sophie while extending the education he intended for Émile to girls and women, we have stopped worrying about whether we are transmitting to anyone that part of our inheritance whose greatest contributors have been women (Martin, 1985).

As for Plato, he may not have valued the cultural wealth he placed in artisan hands as highly as the wealth he gave to his rulers, but he did not dismiss it as most current educational thinkers do. Indeed, like Rousseau, this political elitist had a broader, more inclusive view of a culture's wealth than do educators now.

So here is the problem. On the one hand, to settle for the goal of one education for all opens the door to a compulsory curriculum, turns dependency into a liability, and does a grave injustice to succeeding generations by failing to pass down to them large portions of the culture's accumulated wealth. To those past generations that amassed the wealth in the expectation that it would be preserved and transmitted to their children and their children's children, it is also unjust. On the other hand, even to contemplate a policy of curricular difference is to raise the specter of elitism.

Look at education from a cultural perspective and one can see that a system of distribution faces two distinct challenges: that of avoiding inequality and that of transmitting as many assets and as few liabilities as it can. Suppose that the minimizing of liabilities part of this second challenge is solved to everyone's satisfaction. The problem would still remain of finding a way to transmit to the next generation a more democratic, in the sense of more inclusive, portion of our superabundant cultural wealth than the policy of one education for all admits *without sacrificing the ideals of political democracy and social equality.*

I call this last "the new problem of curriculum." Admittedly it is an old problem, but so far as I am aware its double aspect has not to date been made explicit. Would that "Cut the trivia" could solve this new/old problem. But those portions of cultural wealth that are now at risk of being squandered are precisely the ones that have given rise to claims of triviality in the first place. I once asked a political theorist teaching at an eminent university if she discussed any women thinkers in her courses. "After I cover Plato, Aristotle, Machiavelli, Hobbes, Locke, Rousseau, and Marx, there's just no time left for people like them," she said. Female philosophers, African American poets, non-Western art: One of the legacies that past generations bequeathed to my generation and that my generation has tried valiantly to pass along to its young is that whatever does not belong to the Western canon is trivial by definition.

Whenever I point out the superabundance of cultural wealth, someone assures me that the problem it poses would take care of itself if only we would pass down to our young the skills and dispositions of learning how to learn. Of course we can't teach everything, they say. But if we taught everyone to learn for themselves whatever they wanted and needed to know, the new problem of curriculum would take care of itself.

Would that this simple answer to the old curriculum question of what to teach could do the trick! But why suppose that those who learn how to learn will have the desire or feel the need to acquire the cultural wealth now being squandered? Why suppose that they will seek out portions of wealth that they do not know exist? And why suppose, in any case, that the skills and techniques that a learning-to-learn curriculum would transmit would apply to forms of wealth that the curriculum developers themselves have been conditioned to ignore? Whatever "the" methods of learning how to learn may be and however many such methods there are, the ones the present generation deems worthy of passing down will be the ones that have proved successful in relation to the acquisition of cultural stock that this generation considers valuable. But then, why think that the methods of learning for oneself transmitted to future generations would be efficacious across the whole wide range of cultural wealth?

Of the two most frequently proposed solutions to the abundance problem, one tries to make the best of the policy of a single curriculum for all and the other takes for granted the ideal of absolute self-sufficiency. The new problem of curriculum is more readily solved, however, if we jettison both assumptions. And the problem needs solving for all the reasons I have given and then one more.

Only while writing this chapter did I perceive the great irony in that publisher's outburst. When he accused me of racism, he was actually projecting the problems of existing educational practice onto the very idea of allowing different people to have different curricula. This man assumed that the only alternative to the policy of one curriculum for all was to design different curricula for different races. And he also took it for granted that the curriculum designed for the dominant race—namely, Caucasians— would contain stock of far greater worth than would those designed for other races. What he neglected to say was that his scenario of future inequalities depicted present realities. He acted outraged at the exploitation and inequality that he was projecting onto a policy of different curricula for different people. The fact that people in our society were already being subjected to very different and unequal curricula did not seem to faze him.

To put the point bluntly: In the names of democratic citizenship and social equality, the United States as a culture tends to preach the principle of the same curriculum for all. Yet our daily practice delivers different curricula to different people—and all too often the recipients' differences are rooted in race or class or gender or all three. Aware of the historical and philosophical links between an educational policy of difference and inequality, we do not care to admit that the exploitation and inequality we attribute to the *de jure* principle of difference is actually a feature of our own *de facto* situation. Never acknowledging the gap between our culture's policy of identical curricula and its practice of different curricula, we do not see that the new problem of curriculum is actually a very old problem. It is also everybody's problem here and now.

THE NEW PROBLEM OF CURRICULUM; OR, LEARNING AS GIFT

When I read Lewis Hyde's (1979) *The Gift*, I remembered the advice my mother once gave me. I had been telling her that one of my friends was forever doing things for me—often big things like giving me rides to and from my parents' home in New York—and I could do nothing comparable for her in exchange. To my great surprise, my mother responded: "You shouldn't feel guilty. It is not always possible to pay back the very person who has done something for you. And she probably does not expect you to. What matters is that at some point in your life you do things for someone else that count just as much to that person as these things do to you."

I do not know where or how my mother acquired her concept of what anthropologists call "the gift"—some call this "the norm of generalized reciprocity" (Putnam, 2001, pp. 20–21) and others speak of "doulia" (Kittay, 1999, p. 107). Hyde, however, took a 1924 essay by Marcel Mauss on the gift exchange in tribal groups as the point of departure for his book. Illustrating the gift with a wealth of examples from the anthropological literature, Hyde listed several of its cardinal properties. One of these is: "Whatever we have been given is supposed to be given away again, not kept. Or, if it is kept, something of similar value should move in its stead" (1979, p. 4). Some possessions stand still. You get something or other and you keep it. But the gift always moves, and although in the limiting case of the gift exchange it may travel between just two people, it normally does so in a circle (p. 16).

A second attribute of the gift is that one person's gift does not become another's capital. Suppose one subclan gives another a pair of goats. The recipients are not expected to give a pair of goats or its equivalent in return. On the other hand, they dishonor the gift and even threaten the fabric of the group if they use the goats they have received to produce milk or more goats for profit. In gift exchange, "the transaction itself consumes the object" (Hyde, 1979, p. 9). This does not mean that the goats must be eaten, although they can be. Rather, "a gift is consumed when it moves from one hand to another with no assurance of anything in return" (p. 9).

All of this adds up to a third feature of the anthropological notion of a gift—namely, that it is not the giver's private property. Philosophers and legal theorists agree that the essence of private property is the right to exclude others (see, e.g., Cohen, 1927/1978, p. 159; George, 1993, p. 391; Mill, 1848/1993, p. 385). By traveling in a circle the gift quickly moves beyond the giver's control. "When I give to someone from whom I do not receive (and yet I do receive elsewhere), it is as if the gift goes around a corner before it comes back," says Hyde (1979, p. 16).

When the subject is the new problem of curriculum, the distinction between private property and the gift is critical. John Locke, the English philosopher whose words about property have often been taken as gospel, wrote that when a person adds his labor to the earth, the result is his property—"at least where there is enough, and as good left in common for others" (1690/1952, sec. 27). So, if you pick up the acorns under an oak or pluck apples off trees in a wood or kill a deer, these goods become your own property. Like Locke's acorns and apples, knowledge and skill tend to be viewed in our culture as the fruits of a person's own labor, which is another way of saying that they are seen as the private property of the one who acquires them.

This "appropriation model" of learning is preserved by school and passed down as living legacy. From day one, school portrays learning as labor. Children have workbooks and do worksheets. When their concentration lags, they are told to get back to work. When they are found chewing gum, they are told, as my son's sixth-grade class once was, that their parents do not chew gum at work and, since school is their place of work, they should not either. Whether the work children undertake in school is reading, filling in the blanks on worksheets, memorizing vocabulary lists, or writing compositions, the idea seems to be that by mixing their own labor with the subject areas of their course of study, the knowledge and skill they acquire becomes their own private property. By no means is this view of learning confined to grade school. University professors ponder the amount of work they should give their students, who, in turn, pay grudging respect to the taskmasters who make them work the hardest—the assumption being that the harder one works, the more cultural wealth one acquires.

A sociologist of education once remarked, "The irony of cheating *in school* is that the same kind of acts are considered morally acceptable and even commendable in other situations" (Dreeben, 1968, p. 68; emphasis in original). He was thinking of everyday demonstrations of generosity, such as sharing one's possessions with family and friends or helping those less fortunate than oneself. As every schoolchild soon learns, kindnesses like these are not supposed to extend to knowledge and skill. In theory, private property is transferable. In school, such largess counts as cheating. What Jerry Donahue did for Watson and Crick may go down in the annals of science, but actions like his would be punished in school if discovered. In school, to acquire knowledge that is not the fruit of your own learning labor is considered at best "a personal foul" (Monje, 1999) and more likely a mortal sin. So is giving another the knowledge that you have acquired through your own learning labor.

Our private property conception of learning is a natural concomitant of the policy that everyone receive the same cultural inheritance. Appropriating for yourself the knowledge and skill you have attained by your own hard work makes perfect sense when there is nobody who can possibly want or need what you have acquired. Why treat learning as a possession to be shared with others when those others stand to inherit the selfsame portion of the culture's stock? A property view of learning is also a fitting accompaniment to the ideal of absolute self-sufficiency. After all, were people to share the knowledge and skill they acquired through their own labor instead of appropriating it for themselves, they would be forgoing the self-reliance that the ideal demands.

We now know, however, that democratic citizenship does not entail absolute self-sufficiency. We also know that this latter ideal is an impossible dream. In addition, we know that democratic citizenship does not require one curriculum for all. We know, too, that this latter policy is not achievable and that in any case the consequences of following a single curriculum policy are undesirable. Finally, and very important, we know that the new problem of curriculum is far more likely to be solved if we adopt a policy of curricular difference.

Prudence would seem to dictate that our culture move the principle of the same curriculum for all from the living legacy end of its preservation continuum to the dead relic end. Or rather, it would so dictate were it not for our present attachment to a private property conception of learning. To opt for a policy of different curricula while embracing an appropriation model of learning is a recipe for exploitation and inequality. When hoarding what one has learned is regarded as the norm, people whose curriculum never did pass down to them the knowledge and skill they now need to perform the tasks of daily life and carry out the duties of citizenship are out of luck.

Suppose, however, that the sharing of knowledge and skill were to become the norm. Then, whatever a person needed to know but had not learned for him- or herself could be obtained from others as a gift. In turn, this individual could circulate to others the knowledge and skill that he or she had acquired through study. It sounds simple, yet to replace the present appropriation model of learning with a gift model will not be easy, for that widely accepted view of learning is part and parcel of the philosophy of social atomism in which many standard practices of American schools and colleges are rooted.

In many schools and even some universities, the old classroom seating arrangement of rows of students facing the front of the room has been abandoned. Classroom conventions governing speaking—you may not talk to your neighbor, you must not call out to a friend across the room—have also been relaxed, and tasks that were once designed for individuals to do are frequently handed out to groups of people. Nevertheless, the individual student is still viewed as a separate being unconnected to others. With each student expected to do most assignments on his or her own and with the evaluation and grading of worksheets, spelling tests, essays, exams, and term papers premised on the assumption of individual authorship, learning continues to be seen as a strictly private affair.

Classrooms would no longer be arenas for the enactment of a philosophy of social atomism—or, if you will, mechanisms for the transmission of such to the next generation—if learning were thought of as gift rather than private property. Picture this: Mark, who loves math, interprets statistical studies for Tony, who is doing a science project on the dangers of cigarette smoking. Tony, a student with a facility for languages, translates several complicated French passages for Fred, who is writing a report on Lafayette. Fred, whose knowledge of history is prodigious, describes Elizabethan England in great detail to Peg, who is reading Shakespeare's historical plays. And Peg offers to edit the paper Mark is writing. This classroom scenario represents the simplest form of the gift in circulation: X gives A to Y, Y gives B to Z, Z gives C to W, and W gives D to X.

Now picture this: Several students are working together on a science project about the dangers of smoking, with each one contributing some body of special knowledge or skill to the group. Here Mark again does the statistical work, but Tony now contributes the necessary physiological knowledge, Fred outlines a history of the discovery and use of tobacco, and Peg does the graphics for the final report. Assume a classroom containing several such group projects and it is easy to see that the knowledge resulting from each one can itself circulate as gift in the manner of our first scenario. Group Q gives the knowledge it has collected on smoking to Group R, Group R gives its findings about the destructive potential of earthquakes to Group S, Group S gives the fruits of its study of IQ testing to Group T, and Group T gives its newly acquired knowledge of the linguistic abilities of gorillas to Group Q.

Does the knowledge that the students in a given group contribute to their own group's project circulate among the group members as gift? I think so. As long as everyone in that group has a sense of belonging to the group, and is so treated, each person's contribution to the group as a whole is also a contribution to the individuals that constitute it. This is not to say that Tony, Fred, and Peg learn the statistics Mark contributes or that Mark, Tony, and Peg master the details of the history Fred offers up. *Giving* the gift of knowledge to someone is one thing. *Teaching* it to that person is something else entirely.

When knowledge and skill are allowed to circulate as gift around a classroom, everything changes. Students begin to move about the room. Furniture shifts in their wake. The norm of silence is replaced by a hum of constructive activity. Communication between students becomes a requirement for successful learning instead of an occasion for punishment. Collaboration between friends becomes a mark of distinction, not a sign of cheating. Helping others becomes a badge of honor. In other words, when a gift conception of learning prevails, a site of social atomism becomes an arena for the enactment of a philosophy of social interdependency

Still and all, allowing the gifts of knowledge and skill to circulate around classrooms will not solve the new problem of curriculum unless they are also allowed to circulate around the "outside" world. So think now about the proliferation of book groups in the United States at the turn of the 21st century. No one would have predicted this grass-roots development. Think about the numerous investment clubs that also sprouted up in that period. Why should there not be a similar burgeoning of public issue discussion groups in which problems such as homelessness, the death penalty, famine, international terrorism, gun control, overpopulation, public transportation, and welfare are investigated and knowledge and skill circulate as gift?

The object of these informal grass-roots groups or organizations might be to arrive at joint policy decisions, in the manner of investment clubs that decide what stocks to buy and sell. Or it might simply be to discuss a set of problems thoroughly while treating their solutions as matters for individual determination. Agendas would, of course, vary considerably. While some groups might wish to concentrate on one problem a year, others might prefer to sample a new problem at each meeting. And while some groups might seek ways of translating their joint decisions into action, others might deliberately shun the political arena. Despite all their differences, however, one distinctive mark of these groups would be that their members possess different areas of expertise, which they share with one another.

Picture this: A public issues group agrees that at its next several meetings the topic will be the homeless. Once this is decided Millicent, an actuary by day, volunteers to collect and analyze the relevant statistical data for the group. Marjorie, a social worker, then offers to survey the social science materials on homelessness. Jeremy, a construction worker, promises to investigate and critique building requirements across the state. Jasper, who once was homeless, agrees to visit local shelters and interview their inhabitants. Henry, a lawyer, says he will review the legal issues regarding homelessness for the group. And Alice, a travel buff, offers to find out whether homelessness is a problem in other countries—if so, how it is handled, and if not, why not.

Now it might be thought that critical thinking is the one area of competence to which a gift conception of learning does not apply. In other words, some might acknowledge that we do not all have to be our own statisticians or economists yet demand that we be our own critical thinkers. Since, however, critical thinking is composed of a number of different elements, one can readily imagine different individuals having expertise in different ones. Suppose, then, that Celeste is very good at spotting fallacies but relatively incompetent at uncovering hidden assumptions or detecting bias, that Ernest possesses one of these other competencies, and so on. If these individuals belong to the same public issue discussion group, the group might well possess the capacity to think critically even if its individual members did not.

Gift-based public issue groups already exist. Assume that a locality contains several and one can easily envision them combining forces occasionally in order to share the outcomes of their separate investigations. Or

rather, one can readily imagine this provided the world outside school
repudiates the atomistic philosophy of social relations to which it is still
wedded. According to Adam Smith, "where there was perfect liberty, and
where every man was perfectly free both to chuse what occupation he
thought proper, and to change it as often as he thought proper," there
would be perfect equality (1776/1976, p. 111). Whether or not one considers his equation between liberty and equality valid, it is well to remember
that he was talking about economic, not social or political, equality. Moreover, in Smith's account, education only bears on equality in respect to "the
easiness and cheapness, or difficulty and expertise" of learning the various occupations (p. 112). Cultural rankings of different bodies of knowledge and skill were not his concern and neither were the culture's attitudes
toward dependency. Yet the sharing of knowledge and skill implicit in a
gift conception of learning assumes the very kind of dependency on others
that social atomism teaches us to despise.

Some years ago another member of the small research group I belong
to and I tried to explain the group's activities to a friend and colleague.
When we told him that we read and commented on one another's papers,
he was shocked. "That's cheating" was his response to the informal institution that we two thought of as life giving. Obviously, we must change
cultural expectations about life in the larger world lest our efforts at implementing a gift conception of learning be thwarted. We must also alter these
expectations lest exploitation and inequality be the unintended outcomes
of circulating knowledge and skill.

AN INTERDEPENDENCY MODEL
OF SOCIAL RELATIONS; OR, SOME
UNRESOLVED QUESTIONS

One ritual I established early in my university teaching career was to read
a passage from Karl Popper's *The Open Society and Its Enemies* to my philosophy of education students on the first day of class:

> It has been said, only too truly, that Plato was the inventor of both our sec-
> ondary schools and our universities. I do not know a better argument for an
> optimistic view of mankind, no better proof of their indestructible love for
> truth and decency, of their originality and stubbornness and health, than the
> fact that this devastating system of education has not utterly ruined them.
> (Popper, 1952, p. 136)

I hoped that the sheer iconoclasm of the diatribe would surprise and de-
light them as it did me. Besides, with half the world condemning contem-

porary education for not following the recommendations put forward in the *Republic*, I wanted them to know that I was not the only one who detected Plato's fingerprints on our educational system. And with the other half of the world delighting in the very educational practices that Popper was damning, I thought it might be comforting for them to know that I was not the only one who thought the master's legacy included stock of dubious value.

The time has come, however, to give credit where credit is due. For Plato is the one who, through his three-track educational system, alleviated the problem of superabundance of cultural wealth. He is also the one who developed a theory of social relations that points us toward a solution of the new problem of curriculum.

Having acknowledged the fact of human dependency, Plato could have proposed an educational system that would minimize or even overcome it. Instead, he built into the Just State of the *Republic* a dependency model of social relations. Perhaps I should call it an *inter*dependency model, for the important point is that the dependency he posited is reciprocal. Even as the artisans are dependent on the rulers for political guidance, the rulers are dependent on the artisans for shoes and ships, as well as for food production, housing, transportation, and all the rest. Like the artisans, the warriors rely on the rulers for overall guidance, yet their dependency is not unidirectional either. After all, the rulers are dependent on the warriors to guard the state.

In view of this give-and-take assumption, it is natural to suppose that the Just State is characterized by mutuality. Yet insofar as the "mutual" label implies the sameness of content of the dependency transactions, it is at odds with Plato's vision. A cobbler who makes shoes for a guardian of the Just State does not expect, and will not receive, a pair of shoes in return. Cobblers know that ruling, not shoemaking, is a guardian's business. Conversely, a guardian who legislates for a cobbler does not anticipate or wish the cobbler to do as much for him or her. It is shoes that the guardian wants and expects from the cobbler. In other words, although in the Just State dependency can be said to be reciprocal, social relations are based not so much on mutuality as on a division of labor.

Now, divisions of labor can all too easily be arbitrary and capricious. Plato gets around this difficulty by adding a postulate of expertise to his postulate of divided labor. Moreover, and very much to the point, the expertise he attributes to members of the Just State derives from the different educations they receive. Thus, the curriculum for rulers is designed to teach the art of governing oneself and others, not shoemaking or shipbuilding. Conversely, the curriculum for artisans is supposed to transmit the knowledge and skills required for shoemaking and shipbuilding, not for the art of governing. Indeed, even as the ruler curriculum teaches this latter, the artisan course of study passes along the art of obedience to those who know best.

As it happens, the three different curricula envisioned by Plato are tailored to the different natures he assigns his three different classes of people. Because in his philosophy human nature is fixed and unchanging, his model of social relations takes for granted the fixity of the content of the dependency transactions. Of course, if people in the Just State were allowed or encouraged to perform tasks that nature and education did not suit them for, the model would not include this premise. But Plato considered the dependency relations unchanging. Perhaps a shoemaker could become a shipbuilder, but no artisan could legitimately undertake to rule and no ruler could switch to food production or shopkeeping.

Citizens of a 21st-century democracy might expect to find unrest or even revolution in a land whose social relations could not be significantly altered. But Plato banked on the fact that people who are raised to believe that they are doing what they were born to do—people who, in any case, always have their needs fulfilled—will not resent their lot in life, not even when it entails obedience to the rule of others. He also made sure that the give-and-take in his system would not be begrudging.

We have all known individuals who like having things done for them but begrudge doing things for others. I, for one, have also encountered people who enjoy doing things for others but feel uncomfortable to the point of being ungracious about accepting what others do for them. The citizens of Plato's Just State have neither shortcoming. His rulers expect to legislate for the artisans and warriors, who, from an early age, expect to be ruled by the philosopher kings. And, of course, these artisans expect to make shoes for the rulers and warriors, who, in turn, take it for granted that whoever has the capability will make shoes for them.

Adapting Plato's model of social relations to his own purposes, Rousseau also joined curricular difference to dependency. It is no secret that their respective educations make Sophie thoroughly dependent on her husband Émile. What is less well known is that in Book V of the volume that bears his name, Émile is portrayed as deeply dependent on his wife. Although over the centuries Émile has been called the very model of an autonomous person, it is she, not he, who will have been educated to manage a household, rear children, and tend the needs of family members. Rousseau also explicitly said that by virtue of their different educations, Émile and Sophie qualify as the two complementary halves of a single moral whole. On his own reckoning, neither person alone is or can ever be a completely moral person.

As Plato identified three main groups or classes in society and made sure that the members of each one were dependent on the members of the others, Rousseau identified two such groups and saw to it that the dependency was reciprocal. Without a doubt, Sophie is dependent on Émile for his guidance of herself and her family and for representing her interests in his capacity of citizen. But Émile would find it all but impossible to carry on if Sophie did not do for him all the things that Rousseau intended her to do. All of which is to say that Rousseau also postulated a division of labor, albeit a very different one from Plato's. In Plato's utopian vision, children are public charges. In Rousseau's, Sophie tends to Émile's children without ever expecting him to return that favor and without ordering him about as he orders her. This is because they both know full well that ruling, not child care, is his business and that child care, not ruling, is hers.

As one might expect, Rousseau's scheme is every bit as grounded in education as Plato's. Émile's curriculum is designed to give him expertise in being his own legislator and Sophie's, too. It does not attempt to teach him to take care of children or to run a household. Sophie's curriculum gives her expertise in these even as it denies her training in self-government. Following Plato's lead, Rousseau assumes not merely that the content of the dependency relation between Sophie and Émile will remain constant but that Sophie will accept Émile's rule of her with grace and will do his child care ungrudgingly, even as he takes it for granted that ruling is his job and that child rearing is hers.

From the standpoint of finding a solution to the new problem of curriculum, this model seems promising so long as knowledge, skill, attitudes, and values are brought within its orbit. The truth is that Plato tacitly exempted these from his interdependency model of social relations. Although he abolished the institution of private property for his rulers, he allowed them to appropriate for themselves the knowledge and skill they acquired through their rigorous education. The rulers provide guidance, commands, and legislation for the artisans. Had he viewed their learning as gift rather than private property, he would instead have seen to it that the rulers give the artisans the information and insights that they need in order to govern themselves. Similarly, the artisans make shoes and ships for the rulers. Had Plato conceptualized learning as gift, his artisans would have given the rulers the knowledge they needed to make such goods.

So now let us extend the interdependency model's orbit to the sharing of knowledge, skill, and other types of learning. And let us then go ahead and substitute a conception of human beings as interdependent for a view of us as unconnected atoms. Once we join this model to the policy of different curricula for different people and to a gift conception of learning, we will be on the right track.

I do not say that we can then sit back and expect the new problem of curriculum to take care of itself, for some enormously difficult questions remain to be answered. The first vexing question on my list arises from the fact that in the interests of democracy we must scrap Plato's thesis that different people are born with different fixed, unchanging natures that suit them for different roles in society. To be sure, Plato acknowledged that a child's nature might differ from that of his or her parents. In addition, it does seem to be true that some talents are inborn. But neither his claim of immutability nor his assumption of a perfect correspondence between natures and society's roles is warranted. Besides, the Platonic thesis supports an elitist political philosophy. Quite simply, in the world of the *Republic*, a person's "inborn" nature determines his or her place in society, and hence his or her curriculum track.

Reject the metaphysical claim about inborn natures and the accompanying deterministic thesis about people's "place" in society and the question is: On what basis, if any, should the culture's wealth be distributed? From the standpoint of the new problem of curriculum, to substitute for Plato's postulate of inborn natures some equally arbitrary basis for deciding who gets which portions of the culture's stock—for instance, race, class, or gender—is unacceptable. Are there any bases other than a lottery that are not arbitrary? And doesn't a lottery—with its disregard for individual talents, interests, and choices, and with its implicit dose of compulsion—simply repeat many of the same problems that plague the policy of a single education for all?

A second challenging question emerges from the fact that our culture has inherited from the ancients a value hierarchy that ranks intellectual labor far above both manual labor and the caring labor that includes child rearing and the myriad other activities that have traditionally been associated with women and the world of the private home. The question for one who wishes to solve the new problem of curriculum is: How can we *revalue* the various kinds of cultural stock so that a policy of different curricula for different people does not entail exploitation and inequality? Since we live in a society that tends to follow the principle that you have only as much social and economic status as do the knowledge and skill you have in your possession, any policy of different curricula for different people is fraught with danger. She whose education gave her expertise in caring for the elderly or for infants is unlikely to be perceived as the equal of him whose education trained him to be a computer scientist or a brain surgeon. He who possesses the knowledge and skill needed to build highways or skyscrapers will also be deemed a lesser individual. How can we redistribute the value attributions that our culture now attaches to different bodies of knowledge and skill? That is the question.

The third question on my list is equally troubling: Is a model of social relations that includes the sharing of knowledge and skill compatible with an economic system in which those with expertise charge high fees for their services? I do not mean to imply that social interdependency precludes reliance on "professionals." People who work collaboratively in trying to decide what actions to take regarding public welfare policy do not become unconnected individuals just because they rely on others to make the shoes they wear and the cars they drive. Interdependency does not preclude their employing an accountant to do their income taxes, a mental health expert to counsel their teenager, a plumber to fix a leak. On the contrary, specialization and dependency represent the keys to a solution to the new problem of curriculum. The issue, as I see it, is not that fees for service conflict with either our model of social interdependency or a gift conception of learning. It is that any economic order that encourages reliance on professionals who charge for their services must also leave ample space for the sharing of knowledge and skill that a policy of different curricula for different people requires.

The fourth question takes us back full circle to the issue of whether there is, after all, some specifiable portion of cultural wealth that must be passed down to every individual. Don't a gift conception of learning and an interdependency model of social relations themselves require the prior possession of certain habits of heart and mind? I hesitate even to raise this question because the temptation to pile up universal curriculum requirements is so hard to resist. Yet the question demands an answer. A gift conception of learning does indeed incorporate a nonpossessive attitude toward one's own knowledge and skill as well as trust in the competence and the good intentions of others and an ability to read character. An interdependency model of social relations does, in turn, entail a willingness to rely on others and to be relied on by them in turn.

Does all of this translate into the very policy I have been condemning—a single curriculum for all, albeit one with untraditional content? Or can attitudes such as trust and a willingness to share simply be acquired in the process of circulating learning and in the course of leaning on others? And suppose that when knowledge and skill are being circulated, an individual refuses to participate—refuses to act as either a gift giver or receiver. Do we then start down that well-traveled road to compulsion and alienation?

I am inclined to say that those who refuse to conceptualize learning as gift or to participate in the interdependency model of social relations should not be forced to. But I leave the working out of an adequate answer to this question—as to all my others—for another occasion.

My fifth and last question—which is not to say that it is the only remaining one—is of a different order. In the case of cultural liabilities, the fact of multiple educational agency is part of our problem. Given the multiplicity of educational agents, how difficult it is to stanch the flow of liabilities! In the case of assets, however, multiple educational agency can be part of the problem's solution. For just as one individual can lean on others for some item of learning, different individuals can acquire that learning from different educational agents.

Even now different portions of the wealth are in the custody of different guardians. But suppose the whole wide range of agents were to take responsibility for preserving different portions of the wealth. And suppose they were to harness the principle of the division of labor to the goal of maximizing the transmission of the culture's assets. And suppose they were also to reinforce rather than sabotage each other's work and even step into the breach when a tried-and-true custodian of the wealth was no longer to carry out its responsibilities. Then a solution to the problem of maximizing our assets would seem to be at hand.

I say "seem" because it is one thing for our educational agents to preserve and transmit as much of the wealth as possible and quite another for them to distribute the wealth fairly. When cooperation among the culture's numerous educational agents is added to the brew of different curricula, a gift conception of learning, and an interdependency model of social relations, the unequal valuation of the various custodians of the wealth comes into play. If some guardians of the culture's wealth are more highly valued than others, won't their beneficiaries inherit the higher esteem as well as the assets in that guardian's charge?

A great deal more needs to be said about the role of multiple educational agency in maximizing the transmission of cultural assets while avoiding the traps of inequality and exploitation. My object here has not been to exhaust the subject but to point in the direction of solutions that are consonant with the principles of democracy. I trust I have made it crystal clear that cultural miseducation is a fact of life. But the superabundance of cultural wealth and the multiplicity of educational agents are facts of life, too. And the cultural-wealth perspective on education that allows these to be seen is readily available to all. Thus the materials are at hand to solve what is surely one of the most important problems that our culture, indeed any culture, faces—the educational problem of generations. They are also at hand to solve what is one of the most important problems that our democracy, indeed any democracy, confronts—the new problem of curriculum. Yes, it will take a concerted effort, the will to make the world a better place for our children, and a little bit of luck. But are these too much to ask?

References

Addams, J. (1990). *Twenty years at Hull-House*. Urbana: University of Illinois Press. (Original work published 1907)

Adler, M. (1982). *The paideaia proposal*. New York: Macmillan.

Allen, P. G. (1986). *The sacred hoop*. Boston: Beacon Press.

Appiah, K. A., & Gates, H. L. Jr. (1996). *The dictionary of global culture*. New York: Random House.

Apple, M. W. (1979). *Ideology and curriculum*. London: Routledge & Kegan Paul.

Aucoin, D. (1998, September 25). Despite vow, many TV shows lack rating labels, study says. *Boston Globe*, p. A14.

Bailyn, B. (1960). *Education in the forming of American society*. New York: Vintage.

Barash, D. P. (1991). *Introduction to peace studies*. Belmont, CA: Wadsworth.

Bart, P. B., & Jozsa, M. (1980). Dirty books, dirty films, and dirty data. In L. Lederer (Ed.), *Take back the night* (pp. 204–217). New York: Morrow.

Beals, R. (1953). Acculturation. In A. L. Kroeber (Ed.), *Anthropology Today* (pp. 621–641). Chicago: University of Chicago Press.

Beattie, J. (1964). *Other cultures*. New York: The Free Press.

Belenky, M. F., Bond, L. A., & Weinstock, J. S. (1996). *A tradition that has no name*. New York: Basic Books.

Bellah, R. N., Madsen, R., Sullivan, W. M., Swidler, A., & Tipton, S. M. (1985). *Habits of the heart*. Berkeley: University of California Press.

Berry, W. (1987). *Home economics*. San Francisco: North Point Press.

Blair, J., & Weissman, S. (2000, April 9). The biography of a gun. *New York Times*, pp. WK 1,18.

Bok, S. (1998). *Mayhem*. Reading, MA: Addison-Wesley.

Bombardieri, M. (2000, May 5). School with no grades catching on. *Boston Globe*, pp. B1, B5.

Carnes, J. (Ed.). (1999). *Responding to hate at school*. Montgomery, AL: Teaching Tolerance.

Carpenter, K. E. (1996). *Readers & libraries*. Washington, D.C.: Library of Congress.

Cassidy, T. (1995, November 1). Let us now raze famous dens. *Boston Globe*, pp. 1, 14.

Chang, I. (1997). *The rape of Nanking*. New York: Penguin.

Clark, B. (1978). *Whose life is it anyway?* New York: Avon Books.

Clark, M. (1989). *The great divide*. Canberra, Australia: Curriculum Development Centre.

Cohen, M. (1978). Property and sovereignty. In C. B. Macpherson (Ed.), *Property* (pp. 153–176). Toronto: University of Toronto Press. (Original work published 1927)

Cremin, L. (1965). *The genius of American education*. New York: Vintage.

Cremin, L. (1968). *The transformation of the school*. New York: Knopf.

Croce, A. (1993, June 7). The Balanchine show. *The New Yorker*, pp. 99–103.

Dawkins, R. (1976). *The selfish gene*. Oxford: Oxford University Press.

Dennett, D. C. (1991). *Consciousness explained*. Boston: Little, Brown.

Dennett, D. C. (1995). *Darwin's dangerous idea*. New York: Simon & Schuster.

Dewey, J. (1934). *Art as experience*. New York: Minton, Balch.

Dewey, J. (1956). *The school and society*. Chicago: University of Chicago Press. (Original work published 1900)

Dewey, J. (1961). *Democracy and education*. New York: Macmillan. (Original work published 1916)

Dewey, J. (1963). *Experience and education*. New York: Macmillan. (Original work published 1938)

Diamond, J. (1999). *Guns, germs, and steel*. New York: Norton.

Dickinson, A. (2000, May 8) Video playground. *Time*, p. 100.

Drake, I. J. (2000, July 16). The many ways to teach a child [Letter to the editor]. *New York Times*, S4, p. 14.

Dreeben, R. (1968). *On what is learned in school*. Reading, MA: Addison-Wesley.

DuBois, W. E. B. (1965). *The souls of Black folk*. In *Three Negro classics*. New York: Avon Books. (Original work published 1903)

Eck, D. L. (1996). Neighboring faiths. *Harvard Magazine, 99*(1), 38–45.

Expanding the vision. (2000). Boston: WGBH.

Foucault, M. (1979). *Discipline and punish*. New York: Vintage.

Foucault, M. (1980). *Power/knowledge: Selected interviews and other writings 1972–1977* (C. Gordon, Ed.). New York: Pantheon.

Fountain, H. (2000, January 30). Now the ancient ways are less mysterious. *New York Times*, p. WK5.

Frankena, W. (1970). A model for analyzing a philosophy of education. In J. R. Martin (Ed.), *Readings in the philosophy of education* (pp. 15–22). Boston: Allyn & Bacon.

Funiciello, T. (1993). *Tyranny of kindness*. New York: Atlantic Monthly Press.

Gardner, H. (1983). *Frames of mind*. New York: Basic Books.

George, H. (1993). Progress and poverty. In P. Smith (Ed.), *The nature and process of law* (pp. 390–396). New York: Oxford University Press.

Gilligan, C. (1982). *In a different voice*. Cambridge, MA: Harvard University Press.

Gilman, C. P. (1979). *Herland*. New York: Pantheon. (Original work published 1915)

Giroux, H. (1981). *Ideology, culture, and the process of schooling*. Philadelphia: Temple University Press.

Gorov, L. (1998, May 22). Ore. youth kills 1, wounds 23 in school shooting spree. *Boston Globe*, pp. A1, A20.

Grant, G. (Ed.). (1996). *The educational life of the community: Outcomes of a metropolitan study*. Syracuse, NY: EDLOC Press.

Greenblatt, S. J. (1990). *Learning to curse*. New York: Routledge.

Groce, N. E. (1985). *Everyone here spoke sign language*. Cambridge, MA: Harvard University Press.

Hacking, I. (1986). The archeology of Foucault. In D. C. Hoy (Ed.), *Foucault: A critical reader* (pp. 27–40). Oxford: Blackwell.

Hart, E. T. (1999). *Barefoot heart*. Tempe, AZ: Bilingual Press.

Hart, J., & Daley, B. (1998, March 26). Students share explanations, anxieties. *Boston Globe*, p. A29.

Harvey, M. (2001). *The island of lost maps*. New York: Broadway Books.

Heilbroner, R. L. (1953). *The worldly philosophers*. New York: Simon & Schuster.

Hein, H. (1990). *The exploratorium: The museum as laboratory*. Washington, DC: Smithsonian Institution Press.

Henry, W. A., III. (1994). *In defense of elitism*. New York: Doubleday.

Herskovits, M. J. (1952). *Economic anthropology*. New York: Knopf.

Hirsch, E. D., Jr. (1987). *Cultural literacy*. Boston: Houghton Mifflin.

Hirsch, E. D., Jr., Kett, J. F., & Trefil, J. (1988). *The dictionary of cultural literacy*. Boston: Houghton Mifflin.

Hyde, L. (1979). *The gift*. New York: Vintage.

Illich, I. (1972). *Deschooling society*. New York: Harrow Books.

Jackson, D. Z. (1989, June 2). The seeds of violence. *Boston Globe*, p. 23.

Kelly, M. (1997, December 4). If Clinton were really serious about cyberporn, he'd prosecute. *Boston Globe*, p. A21.

Kittay, E. F. (1999). *Love's labor*. New York: Routledge.

Koh, E. L. (1999, July 13). Exposing another side of history. *Boston Globe*, p. A3.

Kong, D. (1998, March 25). Children will need reassurance, expert says. *Boston Globe*, p. A12.

Lazerson, M., & Grubb, W. N. (1974). Introduction. In M. Lazerson & W. N. Grubb (Eds.), *American education and vocationalism* (pp. 1–50). New York: Teachers College Press.

Lehigh, S. (2000, June 25). MCAS and me. *Boston Globe*, pp. E1, E5.

Locke, J. (1952). *The second treatise of government*. Indianapolis: Bobbs-Merrill. (Original work published 1690)

Malcolm X. (1966). *The autobiography of Malcolm X*. New York: Grove Press.

Mannheim, K. (1952). The problem of generations. In P. Kecskemeti (Ed.), *Essays on the sociology of knowledge* (pp. 276–320). London: Routledge & Kegan Paul.

Martin, J. R. (1985). *Reclaiming a conversation*. New Haven, CT: Yale University Press.

Martin, J. R. (1992). *The schoolhome*. Cambridge, MA: Harvard University Press.

Martin, J. R. (1993). The new problem of curriculum. *Synthese, 94*, 85–104.

Martin, J. R. (1994). *Changing the educational landscape*. New York: Routledge.

Martin, J. R. (1995). Cultural citizenship. *Boston Review, 20*(1), 15.

Martin, J. R. (1996). There's too much to teach: Cultural wealth in an age of scarcity. *Educational Researcher, 25*(2), 4–10, 16.

Martin, J. R. (1999). The wealth of cultures and the problem of generations. In S. Tozer (Ed.), *Philosophy of education 1999* (pp. 23–38). Urbana, IL: Philosophy of Education Society.

Matsuda, M. J., Lawrence, C. R., III, Delgado, R., & Crenshaw, K. W. (1993). *Words that wound*. Boulder, CO: Westview Press.

McKibben, B. (1989). *The end of nature*. New York: Random House.

Meier, D. (1995). *The power of their ideas*. Boston: Beacon Press.

Mill, J. S. (1993). Principles of political economy. In P. Smith (Ed.), *The nature and process of law* (pp. 383–390). New York: Oxford University Press. (Original work published 1848)

Mill, J. S. (1962). *Utilitarianism, On Liberty, Essay on Bentham*. New York: New American Library. (Original works published 1859, 1863)

Monje, C., Jr. (1999, August 23). Testing consciences. *Boston Globe*, pp. B1, B12.

Montessori, M. (1964). *The Montessori method*. New York: Schocken Books. (Original work published 1912)

Nasaw, D. (2000). *The chief*. Boston: Houghton Mifflin.

Noddings, N. (1984). *Caring*. Berkeley: University of California Press.

Oakeshott, M. (1967). Learning and teaching. In R. S. Peters (Ed.), *The concept of education* (pp. 156–176). New York: Humanities Press.

O'Brien, E., & Rodriguez, C. (1998, May 22). Parents concerned in a violent world. *Boston Globe*, p. l.

Ozick, C. (1987, January 18). The muse, postmodern and homeless. *New York Times Book Review*, p. 9.

Peters, R. S. (1967). What is an educational process? In R. S. Peters (Ed.), *The concept of education* (pp. 1–23). New York: Humanities Press.

Peters, R. S. (1972). Education and the educated man. In R. F. Dearden and R. S. Peters (Eds.), *A critique of current educational aims* (pp. 1–16). London: Routledge & Kegan Paul.

Pettitt, S. (1998). *Opera: A crash course*. New York: Watson-Guptill Publications.

Plato. (1974). *The Republic* (G. M. A. Grube, Trans.). Indianapolis: Hackett Publishing.

Popper, K. R. (1952). *The open society and its enemies* (rev. ed.). London: Routledge & Kegan Paul.

Putnam, R. D. (2000). *Bowling alone*. New York: Simon & Schuster.

Raymo, C. (1999, September 6). Darwin's dangerous de-evolution. *Boston Globe*, p. C2.

Reed, C. (1997, March–April). Biblioklepts. *Harvard Magazine*, pp. 38–55.

Reed, C. (2000, May–June). Picking Harvard's pocket. *Harvard Magazine*, pp. 44–56, 99–101.

Reich, R. (2000, July 11). One education does not fit all. *New York Times*, p. A25.

Robinson, W. V., & Yemma, J. (1998, January 16). Harvard museum acquisitions shock scholars. *Boston Globe*, pp. A1, A12–13.

Robertson, T. (2000, September 3). Extreme TV: Hate groups exploit cable. *Boston Globe*, pp. A1, B5.

Rosenwald, M. (2000, August 28). After 32 years, kindness, tolerance still rule the "neighborhood." *Boston Globe*, p. A3.

Rousseau, J. (1979). *Émile* (Allan Bloom, Trans.). New York: Basic Books. (Original work published 1762)

Rousseau, J. (1947). *The social contract*. New York: Hafner Publishing. (Original work published 1762)

Rule, J. (1983). 1984—The ingredients of totalitarianism. In I. Howe (Ed.), *1984 revisited* (pp. 166–179). New York: Harper & Row.

Saltzman, C. (1998). *Portrait of Dr. Gachet: The story of a Van Gogh masterpiece*. New York: Viking.

Sayers, D. (1962). *The nine tailors*. New York: Harcourt, Brace. (Original work published 1934)

Sayre, A. (1975). *Rosalind Franklin and DNA*. New York: Norton.

Scheffler, I. (1973). *Reason and teaching*. Indianapolis: Bobbs-Merrill.

Sen, A. (1999). *Development as freedom*. New York: Knopf.

Shaw, B. (1998, October). Director's notes. *Parent Bulletin* [Shady Hill School], p. 1.

Shiva, V. (1993). Colonialism and the evolution of masculinist forestry. In S. Harding (Ed.), *The "racial" economy of science* (pp. 302–325). Bloomington: Indiana University Press.

Smith, A. (1976). *An inquiry into the nature and causes of the wealth of nations* (E. Cannan, Ed.). Chicago: University of Chicago Press. (Original work published 1776)

Temin, C. (1993, September 26). City Ballet stars keep the faith. *Boston Globe*, pp. A1, A6.

Temin, C. (1994, March 31). Balanchine's messenger. *Boston Globe*, pp. 61, 66.

Tommassini, A. (1998, August 16). A crowd of old musicals squeezes the new. *New York Times*, pp. AR 1, 24–25.

Tripp, R. T. (1970). *Thesaurus*. New York: Crowell.

Watson, J. (1968). *The double helix*. New York: New American Library.

Watts, J. (1981). Introduction. In R. Lehmann, *The weather in the streets*. New York: Dial Press.

Weatherford, J. (1993). Early Andean experimental agriculture. In S. Harding (Ed.), *The "racial" economy of science* (pp. 64–77). Bloomington: Indiana University Press.

White, J. (1973). *Towards a compulsory curriculum*. London: Routledge.

White, P. (1983). *Beyond domination*. London: Routledge & Kegan Paul.

Wolff, R. P. (1970). *In defense of anarchism*. New York: Harper & Row.

Wollstonecraft, Mary. (1967). *A vindication of the rights of woman*. New York: Norton. (Original work published 1792)

Woolf, V. (1938). *Three guineas*. New York: Harcourt, Brace, and World.

Yanne, L. (1997, February 6). Zoos are teaching children the wrong lessons [Letter to the Editor]. *Boston Globe*, p. A18.

Zernike, K. (2000, June 18). When testing upstages teaching. *New York Times*, p. WK6.

Zernike, K., & Sargent, H. (1998, December 7). A school's outcast. *Boston Globe*, pp. B1, B9.

Index

About the Author

A PIONEER in the study of gender and education and the author of many books and essays on the philosophy of education, Jane Roland Martin is a professor of philosophy emerita at the University of Massachusetts, Boston. The holder of honorary degrees from universities in Sweden and the United States and a past president of the Philosophy of Education Society, she is the recipient of numerous awards, among them fellowships from the John Simon Guggenheim Memorial Foundation, the National Science Foundation, the Bunting Institute of Radcliffe College, and the Japan Society for the Promotion of Science. Martin's most recent books are *Coming of Age in Academe*; *Changing the Educational Landscape*; *The Schoolhome*; and *Reclaiming a Conversation*.